Dreamstealers

How to stop your destiny being stolen

by

Jo Naughton

**Grosvenor House
Publishing Limited**

Jo Naughton is hereby identified as author of this
work in accordance with Section 77 of the Copyright, Designs
and Patents Act 1988

The book cover picture is copyright to Jo Naughton

This book is published by
Grosvenor House Publishing Ltd
28-30 High Street, Guildford, Surrey, GU1 3EL.
www.grosvenorhousepublishing.co.uk

A CIP record for this book
is available from the British Library

ISBN 978-1-78148-766-2

This book is dedicated to Benj and Abi - you're the best children a mum could ask for. I pray that you will each fulfil every ounce of your God-given potential.

Contents

Acknowledgements

Paolo, thank you for believing in me, encouraging me and for being God's tool to mature me day by day.

Dad, thank you for your wisdom and patience in teaching me how to write and to tackle every type of problem - in life and work. Mum, thank you for your unconditional love down through the years and for your friendship today.

Prophet Cathy, thank you for being an A-grade mentor and for your limitless love and affirming friendship.

Tim and Sarah, thank you for investing your time, talents and love in our lives and ministries.

Introduction

The best way to read Dreamstealers is to search for yourself in its pages. Try to identify which sections paint a picture of your life. You may recognise your reflection throughout.

By God's grace, Dreamstealers will help you fulfil your destiny. It will show you some of the obstacles that are holding you back and give you biblical tools to help you overcome them. It is practical and it tells the truth. Please be open and honest as you read. When we accept the truth, it can set us free.

I am amazed how often God has a different perspective to mine about my life and my ways. I think my heart is right and my motives are pure, but God sees deep within. He knows the truth. Ask the Holy Spirit to show you what you're really like so that He can set you free to be your best.

All names (and some details) have been changed to protect the identity of the people mentioned. Bible references are from the New King James version unless otherwise stated.

I believe that you are about to embark on a remarkable journey towards greater freedom, purity and wholeness. As you read, the Lord will meet with you in a wonderful way and take you deeper in Him.

Chapter 1

Who's guarding your heart?

Many years ago, I had the privilege of meeting an incredible couple that God used to lead a powerful revival in South America. Around two hundred thousand young people in one city had given up everything to follow Christ. We chatted as the pair shared their hearts. Their love and dedication made a lasting impact on me. They saw the call of God on my life and my hunger to be used by the Lord so they prayed for me before they returned to their country. They left me with only one piece of advice: guard your heart. I have never forgotten those words.

According to the Bible, it's not your upbringing, your education, your finances, your friends or your family that will determine how your life works out. It's your heart. It decides whether you fulfil your God-given potential, or not. It establishes how your time here on earth will work out.

What do you watch?

I was raised in a quiet, rural area in the north of England. My husband was brought up in one of the roughest neighbourhoods in London. I used to have a relaxed approach to home security, but marriage soon changed that.

We have a host of procedures around our house to ensure it is protected. When we go out, we leave lights on and we speak quietly. All doors have at least two locks and bolts. When we're away, we arrange for people to drop by to check on the place - even stay over. And we have various security lights and alarms.

Every morning, I watch over my son and daughter as they get ready for school. I ensure that they are washed, dressed and breakfasted. I check that their bedrooms are tidy, their school bags are packed and their coats are beside the front door. At night, I make sure that they do their homework, eat their dinner (especially their vegetables), read their Bibles and get to bed at a reasonable hour.

Keen motorists hand-wash their cars. They polish the bonnet, examine the paintwork for the smallest scratch and pay parking attendants to watch the vehicle while they are in appointments. They even keep a close eye on who they offer a ride to, just in case they leave some dirt behind.

Enlightened husbands and wives guard their marriages, setting aside time to protect and improve their relationships. Good pastors watch over their people, strengthen the weak and help the hurting whilst listening to the leading of the Holy Spirit.

What do you watch over? Perhaps it's your children's relationships or your teenagers' education. Maybe it's your career – you're never late for an appointment, you never miss a deadline and you always reach the office before your boss. Perhaps you watch your weight – counting calories and working out. Or you watch over your wardrobe, storing shoes in their boxes and favourite outfits in the dry-cleaner's cellophane wrapping.

Thank God for diligence. We've never been burgled and I'm sure my husband's attention to security has helped. The children are doing well and keeping a close eye on them has been important. If you're hardworking, you're more likely to succeed. Keeping fit makes good sense and watching your wardrobe means clothes look better for longer. It's good to take care of the gifts and talents God has given us. That's stewardship.

But there is one thing that God tells us to watch more than anything else:

> *"Keep and guard your heart with all vigilance and above all that you guard, for out of it flow the springs of life."* *Proverbs 4:23 (Amplified)*

God says that above every possession or talent, and above every relationship or responsibility, we must guard our hearts. We must keep an eagle eye on the state of our souls.

More than you watch over your daughters when teenage dirt-bags are preying; more than you guard your beautiful new car when a low life is lurking; more than you watch over your home, your family, your career and even your own body, God is asking you to take care of your heart. There are three important reasons why we must pay attention to our hearts.

1. Your heart determines your destiny

I love looking at different translations of the same verse to help me understand what God is saying. The New Living Translation says:

> *"Guard your heart above all else for it <u>determines the course of your life.</u>" Proverbs 4:23*

Your heart determines your destiny. The state of your soul establishes what your future will look like. It's not your education or training. It's not your gift or talent - however important they may be. It's your heart that sets your course.

The Bible encourages us to dream, and to dream big. He is GREAT and we are made in His image. This world needs great leaders, great fathers, great mothers, great scientists, great teachers, great doctors, great businesspeople and great ministers. This world needs great people who can be salt and light.

At Christmas, many of us give our children stockings and we look out for stocking- fillers – nice bits and pieces that will pad out the package. They aren't the main gifts. They just bulk out the stocking and help make Christmas more special. When God made mankind, He did not create any of us as stocking-fillers. Each and every one of us is significant. You have great potential: you were made in the image of the Greatest. However, your heart will determine where you actually end up and whether you achieve your God-given dreams.

When we have unresolved issues or hidden motives that drive us, we limit ourselves. While our hearts are full of insecurities or worries about what people think, we hold ourselves back. By contrast, when we are full of love and our motives are pure, our hearts become a springboard.

2. What's inside will come out

The law of gravity says that what goes up must come down; the law of the human heart says that what's inside must come out:

> *"Keep your heart with all diligence for <u>out of it spring the issues of life.</u>" Proverbs 4:23 (NKJV)*

However hard we try to conceal frustration, ignore insecurity, hide hatred or cover up competition, it comes out one way or another. The Young's Literal Translation shines more light on this verse:

> *"Above every charge, keep thy heart, for out of it are the <u>outgoings.</u>" Proverbs 4:23*

On many office desks are in-trays and out-trays. The in-tray is for incoming mail and the out-tray is for your outgoing letters and papers. Our hearts are like our in-tray and our out-tray in one. We need to watch what we let in because whatever it is - junk TV, magazines, unhelpful relationships, negative thoughts or wrong attitudes - will eventually find its way to our out-tray. Our hearts can all too easily fill up with rubbish. Whether we like it or not, our issues will eventually spill out in front of the people around us.

We all know what it's like to be with someone who is anxious or envious. It doesn't take long before their angst or bitterness starts to affect the conversation. If we aren't careful, it has an impact on us too.

"If <u>he that hath the issue spit upon him that is clean</u>, then he shall wash." Leviticus 15:8 (King James Version)

When you are with someone who is harbouring resentment or nurturing a bad attitude, you can sometimes come away feeling horrible. You have been 'slimed' by their heart issues. When that happens, it's really important to get into the presence of God and ask Him to cleanse you. Pray for your brother or sister with love and ask the Lord to bring His healing and cleansing into their life too. Don't judge them though. You don't know what you are carrying around in your heart or what you are unwittingly dumping on your friends. This is the way the human heart works. What's inside will come out, whether we like it or not.

If we are insecure, it will have an impact on the way we behave and relate to others. We might try to hide insecurity, but even the undiscerning eye can spot it. If I have a heavy heart, I may be carrying a spirit of heaviness around with me and making the atmosphere heavy for others. When we're offended, resentment will all too often be on our lips, painted across our faces and evident in our body language. We might think, "I'm just upset or cross". In truth, we're probably offended.

The verse in Proverbs says that out of the heart *spring* the issues of life. The human heart is like a spring or a river. When it starts flowing, it gushes.

The way I see things, we all have issues. The issues that I had to contend with over the years included insecurity, man-pleasing and competitiveness. Insecurity made me crave affirmation, the fear of man made me overly anxious about the opinions of others and competitiveness made me battle with friends to be the best. All of that was exhausting, but I didn't even know I was doing it.

The word issue in the Bible is from a Hebrew root which means a swarm or a mass of tiny animals. It also means discharge and this is exactly what issues are like – an unpleasant substance that can fester and infect.

When God was telling the Israelites how to maintain a healthy, happy community in Leviticus, He talked about people with issues:

"And this shall be his uncleanness in his issue – whether his flesh run with his issue or his flesh be stopped from his issue, it is his uncleanness." Leviticus 15:3

Some people 'run' or spew forth - they eat, sleep and talk their issues. Being around them can be a drain. They are unwittingly spouting their issues and they need help. I think I was probably like that at one time and I am eternally grateful to the people around me for their patience and love.

Others are 'stopped up' or more controlled. Their issues are hidden or buried. They conceal their jealousy or disguise their insecurity with apparent confidence. Either way, issues affect us and others. What's inside always finds its way out.

3. If there's junk inside, it'll defile you (and others)

The passage in Leviticus says that our issues make us unclean. Whether it's judgmental thoughts or wrong motives, offence or stubbornness, our inner issues can defile us.

> *"It's not what goes into your body that defiles you; you are defiled by what comes from your heart... It is what comes from inside you that defiles you." Mark 7: 15, 20 (New Living Translation)*

If a fleeting jealous thought takes root in your soul, it will soon start to infect your attitudes towards that person. Imagine that jealous thought was about someone you love. With a small amount of jealousy now festering inside, you may find yourself being abrupt or resentful. What started out as a tempting thought took root in your heart and wound up defiling you and damaging an important relationship.

The verse in Leviticus goes on to say that whatever a person with an issue touches is defiled. If we don't deal with the matters of our heart, they come with us wherever we go and affect our relationships.

> *"In water, face reflects face so a man's heart reveals the man." Proverbs 27:19*

In essence, I am only as good as my heart so it might just be time to find out what's lurking beneath the surface.

I want to be a blessing to those around me. I want to be my best and I want to do some good. I am determined to fulfil my destiny. That means I must keep a close eye on my heart at all times. By looking after our hearts, we can keep clean and free from attitudes and behaviours that have the potential to ruin our lives.

How do I find out what's inside?

I believed for many years that I was a confident, successful Christian woman. I had a lovely family, a great job and a growing ministry. However, I was riddled with rejection and full of insecurities. It was only as the Holy Spirit started to reveal the contents of my soul to me that I realised how much I needed His healing love. Even though I wasn't aware of my inner issues, they spilled out wherever I went. I was driven, overly competitive, abrupt, harsh, emotional and attention-seeking. The contents of my heart overflowed even though I didn't know what was inside.

The Bible says that "The heart is deceitful above all things" in Jeremiah 17:9. That means that just as the heart is capable of love, kindness and compassion, the heart is also a master at deceit. Put differently, your heart can, and probably does, lie to you. The verse in Jeremiah goes on to say that as well as being deceitful, the human heart is "desperately wicked". That word wicked means twisted. Unfortunately, it's a problem that we've grown up with:

"...the imagination of man's heart is evil from his youth."
Genesis 8:21b

It is normal for people to believe lies about themselves. We aren't used to facing the truth. In fact, one of the qualities that enables a believer to draw especially close to God is being true to self:

> *"Lord, who may abide in Your tabernacle? ... He <u>who speaks the truth in his heart</u>." Psalm 15:1-2*

God values our decision to want the truth. I can think of many occasions when I have given up believing my own PR and chosen to hear what God is saying, often through my husband or other close companions. I used to think that I was always kind and gentle. One day, my husband told me that I was horribly harsh with certain people. I didn't want to believe it, but I had to if I wanted to go further in God. My faults were so secret even I didn't understand them:

> *"Who can understand his errors? Cleanse me from secret faults." Psalm 19:12*

Awareness is the beginning of change. If you are not aware that you have an issue then you will not know that you need to change. It's time to stop believing that we know ourselves better than anyone else. Instead, we need to recognise that there may well be hurt or junk festering in our souls. Faithful are the wounds of a friend. Sadly, not many of us have friends who dare to tell us the truth. If you find one, treasure them and honour them. If you don't have people in your life who will tell it like it is, the Holy Spirit will. If you have the humility of heart to hear and the courage to accept what you are hearing, God can do an awesome work in you.

Just like David, Israel's greatest king, ask the Lord to examine you and expose the issues, pain, motives or agendas within. God will be faithful to bring them to the surface:

"Search me Oh God and know my heart; try me and know my anxieties and see if there is any wicked way in me and lead me in the way everlasting." Psalm 139:23-24

Why am I like that?

There is one other important step. We need to look beyond the symptom and address the underlying cause. If I were suffering from stomach pains that lasted for several weeks, simply taking painkillers would be futile. I would need to find out what was causing the pain and then seek medicine to treat the problem. Paracetamol will never cure an ulcer even though it may take the pain away. However, medication combined with a change in lifestyle will.

If you struggle with jealousy, you need to find out why in order that you can deal with the root and start to think and behave differently. If you have regular outbursts of anger, zipping up your mouth will help, but it isn't a long-term answer. You need to discover what is behind the rage so that you can ask the Holy Spirit to set you free. Likewise, realising that you're insecure is only part of the solution. Discovering how you can be secure in God is what will bring you real peace.

If you want to fulfil your potential and achieve your destiny then I invite you to open your heart as you read this book. Please don't set out with the view that you know yourself completely. You don't. Only God does:

"O Lord You have examined my heart and You know everything about me." Psalm 139:1 (New Living Translation)

Our hearts lie to us and conceal pain and problems. If we want to be free, we will need to be willing to allow the Spirit to show us the truth. We will need to allow the Word of God to be our mirror, revealing our inner issues and attitudes.

This book deals with seven deadly heart diseases. These are common problems that people struggle with in everyday life. Most of us encounter these issues in one way or another. I encourage you to read with an open mind and a humble heart. Ask God to speak to you and to show you a reflection of yourself in His Word. He will bring you on a glorious journey of discovery. As you open your heart and listen to His Spirit, He will renew, refresh and restore you.

Prayer

Father God,

I thank You that You have a wonderful plan for my life. You created me to make a difference and to have an impact. I truly desire to achieve my full potential and to fulfil my destiny.

I recognise that my heart determines the course of my life so I ask You to search my heart. Come, Holy Spirit of truth, and reveal my issues to me. Try me, oh Lord, and test me: examine my inner thoughts, my desires, my motives and my buried emotions. Show me what's inside so that I can be cleansed and freed. Remove every obstacle in my soul and lead me on a journey to greater freedom and purity.

Do what You want to do in me so that Jesus is glorified in me and through me.

In Jesus's name,

Amen.

Chapter 2

Help, someone's better than me!

A basic human need is to feel safe. When we feel safe, we feel secure. From birth, babies seek security. Sitting happily on mum's lap or being held firmly in dad's protective arms, a little child learns to feel secure. Or that's how it should be. Add into the mix turbulence, pain, pressure or dysfunction and you might not have learned what real security feels like. Even loving homes aren't perfect. When the unexpected happens and life deals painful blows, it's not long before insecurity in some measure enters most of our hearts.

What do we do about insecurity?

Insecurity is compulsive. Feelings do not necessarily drive us to action. I can feel happy or sad, but I won't need to do anything about that feeling. However, when we feel insecure, there is an almost irresistible craving for reassurance. This may come from an acknowledgement, a compliment, an achievement or a hug.

Insecurity is a very unpleasant feeling and the natural instinct is to do whatever is necessary to dispel it. If you were walking along a cliff edge and there was a powerful gust of wind, you would reach out to grab the nearest rock. Emotional security is the same. When things happen that threaten our self-belief, we feel wobbly and do what we can to make ourselves feel secure again.

Some people feel the need to always be in a romantic relationship. As soon as one breaks up, you are desperate to find someone new. You don't feel whole when you're alone. You're more nervous than normal. Having a partner makes you feel like you're valuable.

I used to crave success. I learned in my teenage years that doing well could make me feel good. The day I got my school exam results was like a shot in the arm. I did better than I expected and doing well made me believe, perhaps for the first time, that I could be successful. It made me feel important. Every promotion or achievement, every contract won and each compliment from a colleague made me feel valuable. Just knowing I had a job with an impressive title made me feel positive about myself.

I was working as a director in a public organisation when I was headhunted to run a new unit at a leading company. Before I met the person who was offering me the job, my husband prepared me. He said, "Even if he offers you a major pay rise, don't look excited. Be calm and collected." In the event, I was offered more than double my existing salary. When the perks and bonuses were added in too, it was nearly three times what I was earning! I kept a straight face and contained my excitement until I told my husband. But that wasn't the end of it. Just as the company was putting the offer in writing, my soon-to-be-boss told me that they were lowering the salary. It was a significant drop.

That weekend we had a prophet friend round for dinner. I shared the story with him and he responded immediately. "You don't believe you're worth their original offer. Until you do, you won't get it." I didn't value myself the way God wanted me to. I felt like a fraud. I went into prayer and asked Him to restore my self-worth. Within forty eight hours the original offer was back on the table. If you don't value yourself, why should anyone else? The Bible puts it this way in Proverbs 23.7: "As a man thinks in his heart, so he is". That means the image I have of myself will affect my life. In my behaviour, body language and conversation, I will project the value I place on myself. I wanted my salary to make me feel valuable, but I had to know my true worth in God's eyes before I could expect the package I deserved.

I can spot affirmation-seekers a long way off. As soon as you feel insecure about yourself, you go to someone whose opinion you value and try to elicit a reassuring comment. For women, a phrase such as, "Gosh, I'm looking really fat at the moment" is meant to prompt, "Oh no, you look wonderful." "I'm never going to get a boyfriend" is supposed to trigger, "Of course you will, you're gorgeous. Who wouldn't want to be with you?" The compliments come and they alleviate the sense of insecurity. Everything is alright until the next time you feel wobbly again. Then you seek fresh approval to make you feel better once more.

Insecurity drives many people in business. In fact, after destiny, I believe it's one of the greatest motivations.

Maybe you were put down by a parent or humiliated by teachers. Perhaps you were raised in a dysfunctional home where you encountered doubts about your ability or competence at every turn. But you are clever and capable so the desire to prove your brilliance to the people around you makes you do extraordinary things. You are trying to convince yourself as much as others.

If you're from a family with a long line of high performers or if your parents applied a great deal of pressure, it can produce a similar effect. I have watched people hanker after promotions, pay rises and impressive job titles because the position makes the person feel important. Without the title or the last achievement, you don't feel so valuable. In its extreme form, this is one of the reasons why people who lose a post of great influence sometimes take their own lives.

Wendy was raised in a wonderful Christian home, but she knew that she was a 'surprise'. Unlike her siblings, her parents hadn't planned to have her. Although she was well loved, she always felt the need to prove her worth. Wendy strove to be top of the class at school, sought major promotions at work and hankered after public recognition. In church, she made herself useful and held key positions. She became successful in every area of her life. It was only later that Wendy understood how inadequate she had felt. She was healed of rejection and started to receive real assurance and security from God. She realised in her heart and not just her head that she was planned before the foundation of the earth. Wendy ceased striving.

Plugging the gap

Some people seek positions in the church or the world to give them a sense of worth. When we are insecure, being chosen by a leader or pastor to take on an important role can make us feel valuable. When we serve in church – even when we're genuinely motivated by love - we crave recognition for our efforts. If we don't get a special 'thank you' or a 'well done', we go home after the service feeling let down. God might have met you in worship or ministered to you through the sermon, but if your focus is seeking affirmation, the devil can rob the blessing and faith which the Lord planted in your heart.

For some, receiving a personal prophecy from a visiting minister makes them feel valued. You seek a word to reassure you that you are loved and important. If none comes, you go home disappointed and thinking you aren't good enough. The Bible says that prophecy is to edify, exhort and comfort. God knows when we need the prophetic in our lives.

My daughter had medical problems which meant she was in and out of hospital for the first few years of her life. She'd had fifteen operations by the time she was six and I went through it all with her. It was at this time that God started to reveal the condition of my heart to me. I was insecure and had developed a series of coping mechanisms which soon became addictions. These were not to drink or drugs but to people. Even in hospital, I would soak up the attention of doctors and nurses when they treated my daughter. I would deliberately talk about her condition to generate sympathy. My daughter was suffering, but because of feelings of rejection, I unwittingly fed my own need for affirmation through her hospital visits. When God revealed this to me, I was appalled and purposed to break the foul habit.

We develop different strategies or habits to satisfy our craving for approval. You know when you're starting to feel inadequate and so you do something or prime someone to give you your 'hit' for the day. The call from within is, "Recognise my talent, admire my success and show me respect." After someone has told you that you are brilliant, all is well. That is, until the craving builds again and you seek the drug of applause or reassurance once more.

But there are problems with all these patterns of behaviour. We can find ourselves relying on the approval of others rather than the assurance of God. Not only that, our need for affirmation can become the reason we seek a promotion, a pay rise or a position in church.

Insecurity in leadership

Sadly, even church leaders can become reliant on the admiration of their people. They love being loved and find it hard to make decisions that might upset the congregation. They feel insecure about the loyalty of their people and so they say and do things that are intended to stop folk leaving. "God sent you here. If you leave, you will be in rebellion." Or, "You're so important to the ministry here that you can't even think about leaving." If we are secure in God and we believe the church is His then we won't be insecure about how our people feel about us or whether they stay or go.

After a small group of leaders left our church, insecurity tried to knock at my door once again. I felt uncomfortable if anyone asked to speak to me, especially if they wanted to raise a concern. We have always encouraged feedback from our church family. It's one of the best ways we can find out what we are doing effectively and what we could do differently to meet people's needs. But in this season, I was not handling suggestions well. I went to God in prayer and He gave me a wonderful revelation.

He reminded me that it is His job, not mine, to build His church. He took me back to Jesus. One day the Lord was teaching a crowd of His followers and got into some difficult doctrinal matters: "Unless you eat the flesh of the Son of Man and drink His blood, you have no life in you..." Well, His 'church' members were not impressed with that at all, as the Bible tells us:

> **"From that time, _many of His disciples went back and walked with Him no more."_ John 6:66**

They left. All except the twelve, that is. And what did Jesus do? Did He panic, rushing around pleading with the few remaining followers to stay? No. He turned to the twelve and asked them, "Aren't you going to leave too?" Jesus was assured in His leadership. The size of His congregation did not affect His self-esteem. It did not alter the value He placed on His ministry or His significance in the kingdom. He was secure.

The example of Jesus pierced my heart. I sat in the presence of God and told Him, "I don't mind who leaves or who stays! This is Your church and it's Your job to build it, not mine. I only seek Your approval and Your faithfulness. I don't mind what anybody else thinks." From that day, I went back to loving and serving with no strings attached. I reclaimed the security that the devil was trying to steal.

God chooses the weak

When the people of Israel cried out to God for a king, the Lord chose someone who He knew could do the job. But he didn't pick the most confident, assertive man he could find. He looked for someone He could mould into a mighty leader.

God spoke to Samuel about Saul:

> *"Tomorrow about this time I will send you a man from the land of Benjamin, and you shall anoint him commander over My people Israel, that he may save My people from the hand of the Philistines..." 1 Samuel 9:16*

God had all the people of Israel from whom he could choose a leader. But he selected Saul because he had the potential to be great. We know that Saul had insecurities. That didn't worry God. He realised that if Saul would allow Him to work on his heart issues, he would come through the process strong and be His leader.

When Samuel first told Saul that God had chosen him to be king, Saul was horrified:

"Am I not a Benjamite, of the smallest of the tribes of Israel, and my family the least of all the families of the tribe of Benjamin? Why then do you speak like this to me?" 1 Samuel 9:21

He was saying, "I'm big on the outside but small and insecure on the inside. Don't choose me." How many times do we look to our education, our nationality, our family background or our human credentials and think that *they* are what will qualify (or disqualify) us for success? Saul thought that he might have been better placed if he were a Levite or from the tribe of Judah or Reuben, but he was only a Benjamite. In his mind, he was from the wrong side of town, the wrong neighbourhood and the wrong family. God chose him anyway. God doesn't look at your background or your qualifications. He doesn't consider your education or your eloquence. He looks at your heart and simply asks if you would like to be used by Him to do something great.

The Lord was so committed to Saul's success that He orchestrated a public selection process. He affirmed Saul as His choice in front of the whole of Israel. Samuel gathered all the tribes and picked out the tribe of Benjamin. Then he selected Saul's clan and Saul's family until he was finally ready to announce the new appointment. But he was nowhere to be found. Saul was so reluctant to take on the role that he had gone to hide and they had to ask God to tell them where he was!

"Therefore, they inquired of the Lord further, 'Has the man come here yet?' And the Lord answered, 'There he is, hidden among the equipment.'" 1 Samuel 10:22

Saul was insecure about his ability to take on this new role so he tried to avoid the spotlight. Perhaps you don't like being the centre of attention either. The Lord often selects unlikely people. Moses had a speech impediment, Gideon had low self-esteem, Esther was an orphan, David had been written off by his father, Peter was a big mouth and Paul was a poor speaker. I don't know your story, but if God chose people for their abilities, most of us would be disqualified.

I first heard the call of God as a teenager. However, real clarity came in my early twenties when I rededicated my life to the Lord. I was zealous for Him, yet inwardly I was a mess. I had issues of rejection, guilt, insecurity and the fear of man. God called me when I was a mess because He chooses the foolish things of this world to confound the wise. The way He uses weak people to amaze the strong is by making those who were once weak unbelievably strong. He makes those who were once foolish incredibly wise. He makes those who were once hurt wonderfully whole. He turns the world's system on its head.

The Lord chose Saul when he was insecure. It was Saul's responsibility to trust God's choice and to seek reassurance from Him. Saul needed to have faith in God's ability to make him into the man that He wanted him to be. In the same way, you and I need to know that God is able to turn every situation around in our lives. He is able to turn us around and make us whole.

Saul's fix – the approval of people

Tragically, Saul developed a destiny-destroying habit. He looked to people to fix his inadequacy. He sought the approval and assurance of those around him so when the masses questioned God's choice (1 Samuel 11:12), their doubts pierced his heart like an arrow.

Just two years into his reign, Saul made his first big mistake. The enemy was threatening to attack and the people were getting worried. Saul had agreed to meet Samuel at a certain time so that the prophet could sacrifice to God and ask for His favour in battle. But Samuel was late and the people were starting to desert Saul.

This should not have worried the king. God chose him and gave him a prophecy: "You shall save My people from the Philistines." Saul should have stood on that word. He should have believed that promise and said to God in prayer, "This is Your problem! You said You would save Israel through me. The people are afraid, but I know that You will fulfil Your promise. So I'm going to sit tight and wait for Samuel and Your guidance."

When circumstances or people make us wobble, we need to go to God. If events make us feel threatened or insecure, we need to pray. We can remind ourselves of His Word and His prophecies. The Bible tells us to wage war with prophecies (1 Timothy 1:18) and the point at which we most need to contend for the words spoken over our lives is when the world is challenging them.

Saul caved in under the pressure of unpopularity and tried to win back the favour of the people. He sought reassurance from the masses instead of God and he messed up badly. He tried to excuse himself to Samuel:

"When I saw that the people were scattered from me and that you did not come... I felt compelled and offered a burnt offering." 1 Samuel 13:11-12

You and I can build our lives on man's approval or God's. You can either listen to man's compliments or God's Word. It doesn't matter whether you are a king or a cleaner, you will be challenged. Colleagues may criticise your decisions. Your family may question your loyalty. You might flunk your exams, lose your friends or fail in a new business venture. When circumstances or people cause us to falter, we need reassurance from God. We need to go to our Rock - Jesus - and His word to remind ourselves what God says.

Saul's mistake cost him everything:

"The Lord would have established your kingdom over Israel forever but now your kingdom shall not continue." 1 Samuel 13:13b-14

God wanted to establish Saul's kingdom for generations to come. Who knows? If Saul had dealt with insecurity, history may have been rewritten. Perhaps Scripture would extol the qualities and character of Saul rather than David? Maybe we would have worshipped the Son of Saul, not the Son of David? The verse I've just quoted uses the word 'forever'. If Saul had hit the deck and wholeheartedly repented, God might have relented. Rather than changing his ways, Saul only became more preoccupied with the opinions of people.

27

Feeling threatened

I was first promoted to management at quite a young age. My first team included a bright, sparky executive who was an outstanding networker. She could work a room in minutes, leaving with heaps of contacts and goodwill. I wasn't good at this at all. I was a great strategist and an effective planner. However, my 'room-working' skills were seriously lacking. I started to feel threatened by this young woman because I feared that her strength would expose my weakness.

I went to the Lord in prayer about my insecurities and reminded myself that it was God who had given me the job. I soon realised that I had a choice. I could either squash her talent to make me feel better or I could promote her skills and allow her to fly the flag for our team. I sat down with this woman and told her the truth. "You are a better networker than me so I need you to attend all our events and be strong where I am weak." In the end, we both looked good and the team excelled.

Early in Saul's reign, David got a job working for the king and he was faithful in all he did. As a result, the king promoted him and he led Saul's army into battle. God was with David and gave him victory. But Saul felt insecure about David's talent. He thought that David's skills undermined him. I know how that feels. Nonetheless, it's a lie. When God surrounds us with talented people, it's a blessing not a threat. It means that God believes in us. If you recognise that you have felt intimidated by the people around you, I encourage you to bring your fears to God in prayer. You don't need to be daunted by other people's talents. Be glad that God gave you friends and colleagues that you can learn from. Let them be a blessing.

David came back from battle and the women rejoiced in his victory, singing:

"Saul has slain his thousands and David his ten thousands." 1 Samuel 18:7

Saul was like a father to David. When we are secure, we want our sons and daughters to do better than us – to excel far beyond our own achievements. We want our church members to rise high and fulfil their potential. However, if we are insecure, even our own children can be a threat. The Bible goes on to describe Saul's reaction when the people celebrated David's success:

"Then Saul was very angry, and the saying displeased him and he said, 'They have ascribed to David ten thousands and to me they have ascribed only thousands.'" 1 Samuel 18:8

The applause that day was louder for David than for Saul. That shouldn't have mattered to the king. When people wax lyrical about the talents of others, that shouldn't endanger our self-worth. My value is not based on how I compare to other people. It is based on God's view of me. He loves me completely because I'm His child. However, because Saul had relieved his feelings of inadequacy by soaking up people's approval, he couldn't handle it when the praise dried up. He felt threatened and undermined by David. He then became intent on removing his spiritual son from his life.

Attention-seeking

Insecure people often want the pity of others. I used to tell people about my problems. I might mention that my daughter had medical challenges or that I had had a difficult time at work. Pity is a strong emotion that causes people to reach out. The attention and support can make us 'feel' loved. And it can become a fix.

When Saul couldn't get the people to applaud him, he asked for their pity. He wanted his team to feel sorry for him when David was apparently betraying him.

He went a step further. I call it the "nobody loves me" syndrome. Someone says something negative to elicit a response such as, "That's not true, we all love you". When we do that, we are indulging in self-pity, but we may also be trying to manipulate the people around us so that they meet our need for a compliment. Saul told his team that he believed they were all plotting against him:

> *"All of you have conspired against me... and there is <u>not one of you who is sorry for me</u>..." 1 Samuel 22:8*

Saul craved pity and compassion. When he got it, he was temporarily satisfied:

> *"And Saul said, 'Blessed are you of the Lord for <u>you have had compassion</u> on me."' 1 Samuel 23:21*

In the end, Saul's insecurity cost him his own life, the lives of his sons, the kingdom and his God-given destiny.

If we don't deal with our insecurities, they may drive us to make bad decisions. We can end up in the wrong relationships just because we're in need of approval. We can seek a promotion even though it's not God's will. We might avoid confronting our teenager's behaviour because we don't want them to reject us. While we look for affirmation in the wrong places, God will often put our promotion on hold. He wants us to know that we are valuable, irrespective of our position. To be genuinely successful, we need to be able to handle love *and* hate, admiration *and* criticism. For that, we need to be secure.

What's the answer?

David was different to Saul. He looked to God, not to man, for his security. He made a very important decision. Whatever was going on around him, he declared, "The Lord is my rock..." (2 Samuel 22:2)

We see this illustrated vividly in the first book of Samuel. For several years, David was a fugitive who was hounded by Saul's hit men. During this period, David had the opportunity to kill Saul twice. But he refused to harm God's leader and his spiritual father - even though Saul wasn't behaving like one. David revealed the source of his security:

> *"As your life was valued much this day in my eyes, <u>so let my life be valued much in the eyes of the Lord</u> and let Him deliver me out of all tribulation." 1 Samuel 26:24*

Picture the scene. Daily, Saul sought to kill David. Daily, David was on the run from his assassins. Yet when he had the chance to make a demand, he didn't look to the king for promises of protection but to God. David's security was not based on man's opinions. It was determined by what God thought of him. David looked to God to make him safe and secure.

You and I do not need to depend on compliments, recognition, affirmation or anything else to feel confident. All sources of security other than God are like drugs which satisfy only for a moment before leaving us empty and in need of the next reassurance fix. The more an addict feeds a drug habit, the more he needs. So it is with us. If we feed insecurity with any human fix, our dependence on those things will only grow. After you get your shot, your habit is fed and you feel temporarily satisfied. The craving is relieved until insecurity starts to rear its ugly head again.

When we depend on the opinions or applause of others for our security, we are saying, "I am not enough. I am not adequate without their approval. I am not sufficient without my achievements. I am not good enough without that job title. Just me is not enough."

The crux

I believe that one of the most important passages for our security is found in Colossians 2:7-10. Let's look at two verses in detail:

> *"Have the <u>roots of your being firmly and deeply planted in Him</u>, fixed and founded in Him, being <u>continually built up in Him</u>, becoming increasingly more <u>confirmed</u> and <u>established</u>..." Colossians 2:7 (Amplified)*

Rooted. The roots of a tree make it stable. A tree is not affected by passing storms when those roots go deep into the earth. We need to learn that our security can never be based on the quality of our last effort. That will not produce true affirmation because we all make mistakes. Human opinions are often wrong, compliments are sometimes skin-deep and attention or applause soon fade.

We need God's love and His genuine acceptance in order to root us. It doesn't matter how your boss reacts because God's love for you and His confidence in you will never change. If you lose your job (and the title that goes with it), it doesn't need to affect your self-image because you are still a son or a daughter of the King. God never created a failure. Everything He does is excellent. You are not a failure. You're a child of God.

Built up. God longs to establish our confidence and our self-esteem. When we allow people or circumstances to build us, we can also be pulled back down again. But when God's love and His Word build us, nothing can move us. When we understand who we are and *Whose* we are, we can gladly refuse human fixes. When God has built your self-worth, you can endure unpopularity and rejection. You can be certain of your value no matter what people say.

Established. It is God's opinion of us that confirms we are important. We don't need human confirmation of our worth. To be established means to be made firm and made sure. When we are established, we are sure of who we are. We cannot be shaken by man's criticism or opinion. We become sure of ourselves by becoming sure of God's view of us and by knowing who we are - sons and daughters of the Creator. It doesn't matter what others say when we know what God thinks.

Complete. Verse ten changed my life forever:

> *"For in Him dwells all the fullness of the Godhead bodily and <u>you are complete in Him</u>, who is the head of all..."*
> *Colossians 2:9-10*

God is all-powerful, all-knowing and perfect in every way. And you are complete in Him. You and God together are enough. You don't need your friend's approval because you are whole in Christ. You don't need to succeed to feel secure because in Him you are already a success.

As God dealt with insecurity in my life, I started to feel much more at ease wherever I went. I wasn't charged with nervous energy and jumpy around impressive people. I was still a work in progress (and I still am), but I had a greater peace.

However, one person's opinions still affected me – my husband's! One Sunday, I was preaching and God was doing a great work in the hearts and lives of the congregation. However, I could tell that something was bothering my husband. It was written all over his face and in his body language. I continued preaching with all my heart, led a time of ministry and then closed the meeting. I sneaked out immediately after the service and found a private room. I could feel that tell-tale knot in my stomach and the craving for reassurance growing. So I got before the Lord and prayed something like this:

"Lord, You are my everything. You are my all-in-all. I live to please You and You alone. I am complete in You, Lord. I am enough because You have made me enough." Then I lingered a few moments in the sweet presence of my Saviour. All the anxiety and insecurity slipped away as I enjoyed the affirming love of the Lord. I left that room feeling secure and I then ministered to people who were waiting for prayer.

We have a culture of feedback and accountability in our ministry. We are always seeking greater excellence so on the way home I asked my husband if he felt I had done well and what he thought I could do differently next time. As he shared his thoughts about my message, I was totally at peace and learned from his comments. It felt good to be secure.

It is when we hold onto God's opinions of us that we become secure. The applause and approval of people will come and go, but the love and assurance of God will remain forever. Don't allow people's comments to build up your self-image anymore. If man's words build it, they can also tear it down. When people compliment me, I pass their words straight on to my Creator. When people congratulate me, I don't let it build my confidence. I give the credit to God. Whether an endorsement comes from the church, the workplace, your family or your friends, it doesn't matter. Don't build your life on people's opinions. Don't let their words make you feel good about yourself. It's God's job to do that. They will come and go but the love and backing of your heavenly Father will remain constant throughout your life.

When we depend on God, trust in Him, look to Him for our security and allow His Word to build us up, then we will grow.

> *"And it shall come to pass in that day that the remnant... will* <u>*never again depend on him*</u> *who defeated (struck) them* <u>*but will depend on the Lord*</u>*, the Holy One of Israel in truth." Isaiah 10:20*

Our example

Jesus knew who He was and *Whose* He was. He knew His Father loved Him and that He was valuable and important. Before Jesus lifted a finger in ministry, God publicly declared His love and delight in His Son:

> *"This is My beloved Son, in whom I am well pleased." Matthew 3:17*

This is all Jesus needed. The Father's stamp of approval was enough for Him. As a result, He could take criticism and false accusations. He could handle mockery, public humiliation and rejection. Although He was undoubtedly hurt at times, He remained secure through every adversity.

> *"...I know where I came from and I know where I am going." John 8:14*

The Bible tells us that when we receive Jesus as our Lord and Saviour, God the Father loves us in the way that He loves Jesus (John 17:23). As with Jesus, you are His beloved son or daughter and He takes great pleasure in you.

Jesus knew who sent Him and who was with Him through every circumstance of life.

"...I am with the Father who sent Me." John 8:16.

When people undermine or patronise us, we can quietly say to ourselves: "I am with my Father God. He has my back."

Don't react

As God started to reveal the issues of my heart to me, I became more aware of how I reacted to the circumstances and people around me. I went on a foreign trip with a preacher who introduced me to a room full of businesspeople and ministers as: "A pastor's wife with issues." Although I was surprised by the comment, I stayed calm. I smiled and said that I was pleased to meet them all. I was learning not to find a human fix for my needs. I sat quietly and reminded myself, "I am complete in Christ." I didn't feel small. In fact, I felt great. I was dealing with insecurity.

Paul the apostle knew that his identity did not depend on his lofty education or thoroughbred background (which he compared with cow dung in his letter to the Philippians!) His identity was based on God's love and favour. Most Christians misunderstand the word grace and believe it means mercy. In fact, grace means favour. It is hugely helpful to remember this when you read your

Bible. I believe that Paul the apostle was secure in God in part because of this wonderful revelation:

> *"...I am what I am by the favour of God..." 1 Corinthians 15:10*

God favours you. He designed you and He delights in you. You are fearfully and wonderfully made. You don't have to be like anyone else. You don't need anyone's approval because you are already approved by God. When all this starts to sink in, you can begin enjoying security in God.

> *"The Lord did not set His love on you nor choose you because you were more in number than any other people, for you were the least of all the peoples; but because the Lord loves you..." Deuteronomy 7:7-8*

It is not because you are clever, educated, raised in a good home, or from the right class or background. It's not because you look right, sound right or behave the right way that He chose you. It's just because He loves you. You don't need to strive for God's acceptance. You already have it because you are His.

Chosen

At my primary school, the sports teacher had a process for creating teams. He chose captains first and they would take turns to pick team members until the whole class had been selected. I was normally one of the last to be called out. That's not being chosen - that's being tolerated! God does not tolerate you. He chose you before He made the earth. He picked you because He loves you. He was the One who made you and designed you and He has a wonderful purpose for your life. God had a choice and He selected you to be His special treasure:

> *"...the Lord your God has <u>chosen you</u> to be a people for Himself, a special treasure..." Deuteronomy 7:6b*

You can replace the word people with 'son' or 'daughter'. He has chosen you to be His own special son or daughter. Once you accept Jesus as your Lord, your position in His family is settled. You're His.

> *"But you are a <u>chosen</u> generation, a royal priesthood, a holy nation. <u>His own special</u> people..." 1 Peter 2:9*

He chose you and you are special to Him. Perhaps you have a favourite outfit or a well-loved gadget. I'm sure, like me, that you treat your treasured belongings well. That's a tiny indication of God's heart towards you.

Husbands and wives

Many years ago, my husband went on a trip to the Far East with an important minister. When one of the conference sessions came to a close, my husband and this minister made their way to the 'green room' where speakers could have something to eat. As they were chatting, a famous preacher came to say hello. The minister introduced my husband to this renowned speaker like this: "Meet pastor Paul. His wife is successful".

That experience could easily have knocked my husband's confidence and wounded his self-worth. He could have returned from that trip and started to put me down. He could have sought every opportunity to knock my confidence in retaliation or perhaps he might have just withdrawn his affirmation. This happened at a time when I was still the 'walking wounded'. I had not yet received the healing love of God in my life. If he had been cold towards me, it might have finished me off.

Instead, my husband came home, continued to love me and told me about that meeting. Although he was a little surprised by the unusual introduction, he was unmoved. We thanked God that day for his security in God and for the call on his life. I have no doubt that a similar experience could have derailed many men of God and become the doorway to division and competition in marriage. His security quite possibly saved his destiny, my destiny and our marriage.

I am so sad when I see a man who is threatened by the achievements or talents of his wife. The Bible says that the wife is the glory of the husband. That means that a glorious wife is at least partly the product of a husband's love and care. I know that I am a hundred times the woman I was when I met my husband. His belief in me and his kindness and attentiveness have caused me to bloom beyond measure. It was so much easier to believe in myself because my husband did too.

On one occasion, my husband and I were on a ministry trip in South America and we were travelling with a younger couple. I was comparing my husband's dazzling gift for learning new languages with my own difficulties - even with accents and dialects. As we chatted, my husband piped up with a glint in his eye, "That's right.

My wife only speaks two languages: English and rubbish!" We all laughed and I thought no more of it. A little later on our journey, the young lady we were travelling with asked me how that comment had made me feel. I smiled and explained that I am secure in the love of God and in the love of my husband. She was amazed and admitted that such a remark would have left her reeling with embarrassment.

We need to reach a place where we can have fun and laugh at ourselves. We need to get to a stage where we don't need anything to make us feel good because we already know that we are complete in Christ.

When you're secure...

You can laugh. People can laugh at you (as well as with you) and you are at ease. You don't feel the need to defend yourself or retaliate. And you can laugh as well. "Sarah said, 'God has made me laugh and all who hear will laugh with me.'" Genesis 21:6

You can endure humiliation. People can put you down and even publicly humiliate you, but you remain at peace because their actions and words don't determine your self-worth. You're secure. "Then they spat on Him, and took the reed and struck Him on the head. And when they had mocked Him, they took the robe off Him, put His own clothes on Him, and led Him away to be crucified." Matthew 27: 30-31

You can shine. You can be around people who are cleverer, stronger, better looking or more important than you and you are at peace. You are at ease with who you are. Other people's talents and brilliance don't threaten you because you know for sure that you were wonderfully made by God (Psalm 139:14). "I am what I am by the favour of God." 1 Corinthians 15:10

It feels good to be secure. It takes away a host of worries and removes a great deal of angst. It's a process, but it's worth it. I encourage you to stop letting anything build you up except the Lord. Make a decision that God is your Rock and that you will seek affirmation from Him alone. Take time to meditate on His love for you. Come to God in prayer and tell Him that you believe what His Word says. Tell Him, "I'm complete in You. You love me and You accept me so that means I'm loved and accepted. You chose me because You love me. I am Your special treasure."

When you detect the tell-tale signs of insecurity, take a moment to remind yourself that your security comes from God. Leave the room for a minute and quietly go to the Lord in prayer and say to yourself, "I am complete in Him. Jesus and me together, we are enough." Declare that, "I am what I am by the favour of God."

Prayer

Dear Lord,

I can see that I have often felt insecure. I have looked to *(tell God exactly what your fixes have been - job titles, compliments, success, reassurance)* to make me feel important and valuable. I ask You to help me end my dependence on anything except You. I look to You alone for my security. I ask You to forgive me for seeking affirmation in all the wrong places.

I thank You that I am complete in You. I thank You that You are my Rock. I put my trust in You once again. I look to You to keep me safe and secure.

I thank You that You made me in Your image. I am Your child and You are pleased with me. I am what I am because of Your favour.

My true security is in You and You alone. I give You praise and glory!

In Jesus's name,

Amen.

Daily confessions to help you become secure in God

You might find it useful to confess these Bible verses over your life. Personalise them so that instead of saying, "It is He Who has qualified us, making us fit and worthy and sufficient," you confess in prayer, "God has qualified me, making me fit and worthy and sufficient!"

"It is He Who has qualified us, making us fit and worthy and sufficient..." 2 Corinthians 3:6 (Amplified)

"You are complete in Him, who is the head of all." Colossians 2:10

"Whoever listens to me... will be secure." Proverbs 1:33

"The Lord your God has chosen you to be a people for Himself, a special treasure." Deuteronomy 7:6b

Chapter 3

But what will people think?

It's almost impossible to separate insecurity from the fear of man. You might think that you aren't afraid of anyone. However, as you read, allow the Holy Spirit to open your eyes to one of the most common problems of the human heart.

When you are insecure, it's easy to end up becoming a man-pleaser as well. My way of dealing with insecurity was to seek the approval of people around me.

I have met very few folk who are completely free from the fear of man. I could count on one hand the people I have come across who really don't care what others think, but my husband is one of them.

No matter who it is, he doesn't mind. Of course, he values the love, friendship and companionship of those whom God has placed in his life. Yet he doesn't care if his choices, beliefs or views upset, offend or aggravate others. He shows respect to people in authority and doesn't speak out of turn. Nonetheless, he will quite happily tell important figures what he thinks if they ask for his opinion. He just doesn't mind what anyone thinks of him. In all the years I have known him, he never has.

That sounds great, of course, but it used to be a huge problem for me! After insecurity, my biggest problem was people-pleasing. I cared far too much what others - particularly important ministers - thought of me. Meanwhile, my husband didn't mind what anyone thought. As a consequence, some of the most stressful times for us were at Christian conferences. I would be incredibly edgy, watching what I said and trying to cover up for what he said! He would feel exhausted after two or three days of being with an irritable and controlling wife. Strangely, it was only when I was free from man-pleasing that I could see how anxious and bound I had been.

It wasn't just preachers that I wanted to please. If I was with successful friends or relatives, I wouldn't be much better. As nervous energy built up, my arms would go flying - knocking people's drinks over as I told exaggerated stories. Impressions were everything so I would go home after dinner parties worrying about what I'd said and how I'd said it. I'd be concerned that I'd talked too much or been too loud. I would wish I wasn't quite so noisy and often purpose to be quieter in future. I longed to be the subtle, quiet type - even just for a night!

Then there were the people who I looked to for approval. If I was leading a discussion at work or a group at church, I would always be conscious of what certain people thought. Just as a thermometer registers the temperature in a room and the mercury rises or falls accordingly, I would monitor the reactions and facial expressions of key individuals. I'd always check for their approval and consent.

The Bible has lots to say about man-pleasing. Let's look at some important verses:

> *"Fearing people is a dangerous trap, but trusting the Lord means safety." Proverbs 29:25 (New Living Translation)*

Fear covers a very wide spectrum of emotions. This verse is saying that worrying about what people think, nervousness around certain individuals, wariness of some folk, concern about others' reactions or opinions, apprehension, the jitters, dread or outright panic around people are all a dangerous trap.

When we are trapped, we are pinned down, hemmed in and constrained. It's a horrible experience. We can't relax and be ourselves for fear that we will project the wrong image, give a bad impression or upset someone important. When we're trying to please people, we can't live our lives in freedom. Fear tries to dictate who we speak to, what we say and how we say it. The Message Bible puts it like this:

> *"The fear of human opinion disables; trusting in God protects you from that." Proverbs 29:25*

The spirit of fear always seeks to control us. Fear isn't something that we can accommodate without it hampering our lives or behaviour in one way or another. If we are concerned about what people think, that anxiety will control our behaviour around those people. The enemy knows that if he can keep us afraid, he can constrain us. He can stop us doing what we have been designed by God to do. Let's look at verse twenty six:

"Many crave and seek after the ruler's favour, but the wise man (waits) for justice from the Lord." Proverbs 29:26 (Amplified)

Have you ever noticed that the Bible sometimes uses language or phrases that don't come up very often in conversation today? For example, the well known verse in Matthew 6:33 says, "Seek ye first the kingdom of God and all these things shall be added unto you." But what does it mean to seek first? It doesn't mean look for, although that's the way we tend to use the word 'seek' today. If you look up the definition of the words in that verse, you will discover that the Bible is teaching us to *prioritise* our relationship with God – through Bible reading, prayer, church and so on – and that as we do, He will bless us with what we need. Sometimes we have to dig deep in God's Word to find out what it means for our everyday lives.

Let's look at the meaning of some of the words in Proverbs 29:26:

> **Many** – is an obvious word but it's still worth unpacking. It means great numbers or multitudes of people. So this verse is talking to lots and lots of us. It's addressing the vast majority of Christians and most of the people reading this book. When the Bible makes a generalisation like that, I assume that God's Word is probably talking to me and I make a point of listening.

> **Ruler** – the leader, person in charge or the dominant individual. This might not be a king or a governor for you but that person who dominates your world,

whose opinion means a great deal. It could be your boss, your pastor or your leader. It could be a husband or wife, friend or relative. It's that individual whose presence you are always aware of, whose expressions you notice and whose approval you seek.

Favour – means approval, admiration or consent, but the literal word is face. Have you ever looked to see how someone is reacting? You know that if they nod in agreement or smile with approval, you have their support. If they wince or frown, tension builds.

This verse is explaining that many of us crave the approval of a particular person or certain people. For some, it's your husband. For others, it's your father or mother. For many, it's a leader in church or a boss at work. You look for their reaction, their acceptance and their favour. You think that if that person supports you, all will be well. You will be able to achieve your goals and life will be that bit easier.

All too often, you end up being intimidated in your own mind by that person. The intimidation is unpleasant so you try to alleviate it by pleasing your 'ruler'. The person probably has no idea that they have such undue influence over you. In a small number of cases, they will know and may even exploit your fear.

If your dominant person is happy, then the intimidation or fear is kept at bay and all is well. However, when they disapprove or are unimpressed, your stomach knots and tension rises. If you think they don't support your decision or suggestion, you will try to please them in order to relieve the angst. When we are compelled to please someone, we wind up being easily controlled by the enemy. Any suggestion that they are upset causes us to become putty in Satan's hands. Remember, the Bible says that most of us go through these sorts of patterns in everyday life.

When we seek to please people to make us feel at peace, we are putting our trust in man. When we look for our leader's approval to give us confidence, we are turning to people for inner strength. When we draw assurance from family or friends, we are leaning on the arm of flesh. However, the verse in Proverbs says that it's when we trust in the Lord that we will be safe. Safe means secure, protected and cared for. When you and I make a deliberate decision to trust God and to take our eyes off people, He will keep us safe.

Why not look to the Lord for *His* approval instead of that of your boss? Why not check what God thinks of your behaviour instead of your father? The opposite of fearing man is trusting God. You can't be facing north and south at the same time. It's the same with fear. You and I can't worry about people's opinions and trust God simultaneously. God is more than able to take care of you. He'll protect you and stick up for you. He'll favour you and promote you. He'll bless you as you put your trust in Him.

Proverbs 29:26 goes further. It says that justice for man comes from the Lord. What does that mean? When you look to God for approval and protection, He will ensure that you obtain the right outcome in your situation and

He will give you the favour you need for your destiny to be fulfilled.

Man-pleasing in ministry

The enemy always targets men and women in ministry. If the devil can intimidate you, he may be able to prevent you from doing what God has called you to do. If pastors worry that speaking the truth will offend their congregation, they might not bring loving correction. If a home group leader wants to be popular, they may avoid challenging inappropriate behaviour. If a prophet wants to be liked, they could find it difficult to bring the uncompromising Word of God.

"Do not be afraid of their <u>faces</u> for I am with you"
Jeremiah 1:8

"Do not be afraid of their <u>words</u> or dismayed by their <u>looks</u>." Ezekiel 2:6b

At the outset of their ministries, God told two mighty prophets that they could not afford to be afraid of people's reactions. He told them to take their eyes off the crowds and on to their Creator.

Perhaps you have never stopped to reflect on how you respond to the reactions of others. Many of us change our story, re-think our opinions or even adapt our behaviour when we think that people around us don't like the stance we have adopted. It might be subtle, but for some it's a lifestyle. God told these men not to worry what leaders might say or what the masses thought of them.

Take that look off your face

The Lord was specific. He told Jeremiah and Ezekiel not to be intimidated by the looks on people's faces. It's amazing how much you can communicate with a warm, friendly smile or an encouraging nod. God wants our facial expressions to bless others. Unfortunately, if we're unsure of ourselves, we can end up seeking the smiles or nods of others for reassurance. When we're looking for positive affirmation, negative expressions like frowns or glares can be debilitating. God told his servants not to be moved or concerned when people looked cross or unimpressed.

Words of approval

It's not just facial expressions that can intimidate. What people say can render us powerless if we're not careful. God knew that His prophets had to learn to do the right thing even when people around them were telling them that they were doing the wrong thing.

Folk will say all sorts of things about you. They will judge your motives, accuse you of lying, question your purity and mock your love for the Lord. There is no doubt that if we allow everyone's words into our hearts, there will be some that hurt us.

I don't build my self-esteem on people's opinions. I don't allow compliments to penetrate my heart very often. I am very careful about what I receive. People's opinions used to be like a drug to me. I lapped up words of affirmation like a cat with milk. If they said I was great, I felt great. So like a recovered alcoholic who won't go near alcohol, I don't allow myself to feed on words.

> *"Do not take to heart everything people say..."*
> *Ecclesiastes 7:21*

Whether they are words of praise or of criticism, I always aim to push the remarks upwards. When people celebrate my successes, I give glory and recognition to God. Even when people encourage me, I watch my heart so that I don't allow that to build my confidence. I believe it keeps me safe from feeding on man's approval. Jesus said: "I do not receive honour from men." (John 5:41). I am careful to receive honour, reassurance and confidence from God alone.

Similarly, when people condemn me, I give it to Jesus. If we are to grow in God, we have to believe His words more than those of imperfect people. When you have learned to be unmoved by others' opinions, you will be well on the way to overcoming fear.

> *"Thus says the Lord, 'Do not be afraid of the words which you have heard...'" 2 Kings 19:6b*

Some words are sent by Satan to intimidate us, to stop us believing God and to put us down. We need to throw them back in the devil's face. Ignore what the enemy is saying and declare God's Word over your life. For example, if a voice in your head claims that you're not good enough, you can remind yourself of God's declaration that you are complete in Him and fearfully and wonderfully made.

The cost of man-pleasing

We examined Saul's insecurities in chapter two, but as we saw at the start of this chapter, there is a close link between insecurity and man-pleasing. Out of insecurity, Saul sought popularity rather than the approval of God. During his reign, he made two bad decisions and both mistakes were down to fear. He never conquered that crippling feeling of angst or that yearning for approval. Wisdom is the ability to learn from other people's mistakes. My prayer is that we can learn from Saul's.

Rather than trusting God's promises and His ability to deliver and save, Saul panicked.

> *"When I saw that <u>the people were scattered from me</u> and that <u>you did not come</u>... I felt compelled and offered a burnt offering..." 1 Samuel 13:11-12*

Saul relied on the approval of the people and the reassurance of his mentor, Samuel. He had never learned to draw his sense of adequacy from God. As a result, the fear of man drove him to cross a serious ceremonial boundary and conduct an unlawful sacrifice. That mistake cost him his sons' inheritance. Rather than passing his crown down from son to grandson and so on, it ended with him.

On another occasion, God instructed Saul to attack and destroy the Amalekites and everything they had. However, Saul's army wanted to keep the booty and the king consented. When challenged by the prophet, we hear the same old issue controlling Saul again:

"Then Saul said to Samuel, 'I have sinned, for I have transgressed the commandment of the Lord and your words, <u>because I feared the people and obeyed their voice.</u>'" 1 Samuel 15:24

This time, the judgement went further. God told Saul that He would tear the kingdom from him while he was reigning and give it to his neighbour. The Lord dismissed a leader who wouldn't confront his fear of people and gave the kingdom to someone who wanted to please God more than man.

When Samuel told Saul that God had rejected him, he should have hit the ground, apologised to the Lord and cried out for mercy. We know that God responds to heartfelt repentance. He changed his mind concerning the fate of Nineveh when its king and people repented. God rethought David's punishment for adultery and murder after David humbly acknowledged his sin. Who knows? Maybe God would have given Saul another chance.

However, even at his point of downfall, Saul's concern was, "What will people think?" He asked Samuel to accompany him back to town, giving the impression to the elders and the masses that all was well.

"Please honour me now before the elders of my people and before Israel and return with me..." 1 Samuel 15:30

Samuel went with him. However, he was broken-hearted that the leader he loved and mentored threw away his destiny because he wanted people to like him.

If you know that you have hankered after the approval of people or worried about man's opinions, I encourage you to start a wonderful journey to freedom. It might be one particular person whose opinion means too much. Make the decision to change your ways today. You and I don't need to look to people for our confidence. We can draw our affirmation from God. We can break the horrible habit of man-pleasing and instead enjoy a liberated lifestyle of seeking God's pleasure.

In the spotlight?

Leaders - in the church and marketplace - can be especially susceptible to man- pleasing because they are in the spotlight and attract more attention. If you know God has called you to any level of leadership, search your heart.

"Even among the rulers many believed in Him <u>but because of the Pharisees they did not confess Him</u> lest they should be put out of the synagogue; <u>for they loved the praise of men more than the praise of God.</u>" John 12:42-43

Do you enjoy praise? Does it make you feel good? If you are a speaker or a business leader, do you get a buzz out of positive feedback? If you are a worship leader or a singer, do you feel great when people applaud your efforts? If you are an entrepreneur or a successful consultant, do you enjoy admiration? Man-pleasing is a slippery slope and many have fallen from the favour of God by seeking the praise of people.

When you enjoy pleasing God instead, you place your life in His hands. He gives you favour for your destiny to be fulfilled. Saul tried to protect his position by seeking the approval of the people and he lost it. David sought to please God and so God protected him, gave him a position and favour with the people.

> *"Now all the people took note of it and it pleased them since whatever the king did pleased all the people." 2 Samuel 3:36*

The effects of fear

When we are afraid of people and seek the approval of those around us, it has a greater impact on our everyday lives than we know.

> *"For God did not give us a spirit of timidity (of cowardice, of craven and cringing and fawning fear) but (He has given us a spirit) of power and of love and of a calm and well-balanced mind and discipline and self-control." 2 Timothy 1:7 (Amplified)*

Why do you think God tells us that, instead of fear, He has given us power, love and sound thinking? Because fear robs us of all three!

> **Power** – if you don't deal with fear, it renders you powerless to obey God, powerless to stand up for what you believe, powerless to honour God and powerless to say and do the right thing. When you're free from fear, you have the power to make the right choices and follow your heart.

Love – when fear dominates, love cannot have its way in your life. If you're worried about what someone thinks, you might not contradict their opinion in support of someone weaker. When you are afraid of people, you can't be patient or kind. You end up being compelled to alleviate the intimidation. "He who fears has not been made perfect in love." (1 John 4:18b). When you're free from fear, love can flow through you to others and bring them joy and healing.

Sound thinking – when you're desperate to please people, it clouds your judgment and overrides sensible decision-making. You lose your peace and you can't think logically. When you're free from fear, you're able to judge what's best. You can make the right decisions, irrespective of what other people think.

Fear is an enemy of power, love and sound thinking. If you need God's power at work in your life, if you long to walk in love, if you want to be a clear thinker - it's time to conquer fear.

We must stop kidding ourselves that man-pleasing is an expression of honour. When you honour someone, you don't need them to be pleased with you. If you find it hard to say no, if you struggle with disappointing people when God is leading you in a different direction, if you always want everyone to be happy, you probably have an issue with the fear of man.

Set free

Thank God that freedom is available to every one of us. It might take a step of faith and an act of boldness at the beginning, but the wonderful sense of liberty makes all that worth it!

"Listen to me, you who know right from wrong, you who cherish my law in your hearts. Do not be afraid of people's scorn, nor fear their insults." Isaiah 51:7 (New Living Translation)

You don't have to allow the fear of what people might say or think to affect your decisions any longer. You don't need to let the longing to be liked or respected, or to be valued or loved, influence your behaviour anymore. It's called man-pleasing and it spoils lives.

"Who are you that you should be afraid of a man who will die?" Isaiah 51:12b

It's not right that a son or daughter of God should be constrained by the opinions of imperfect people. Why should you put up with fear any longer? It's awful to be constantly worrying what people think or to be intimidated by someone.

When God was instructing Paul the apostle about his mission, he made a very interesting statement:

"I have appeared to you for this purpose to make you a minister... I will deliver you from the Jewish people, as well as from the Gentiles to whom I now send you to open their eyes, to turn them from darkness to light, from the power of Satan to God..." Acts 26:16-18

He told Paul, "I will deliver you from the people." If we are to lead others, we must be delivered from their opinions and approval. If you desire to be an influencer in the church or the world, ask God to deliver you from every person to whom He sends you. We can't minister effectively to people we want to please. It's only when we are delivered from their opinions that we can bring light and truth into their lives.

Please God

Jesus is our standard. He made a vital decision right at the start of His ministry:

> *"...I always do those things that please Him." John 8:29b*

When there is a choice to make, follow God. If you want the Lord to use you to do something special, if you desire to fulfil your God-given potential, you will have to stop seeking man's approval:

> *"Now am I trying to win the favour of men or of God? Do I seek to please men? For if I were still seeking popularity with men, I would not be a bondservant of Christ" Galatians 1:10*

Being a servant of Christ means that we must seek to please Him alone. Popularity will come and go. Approval and praise will peak and fade. But God's favour lasts a lifetime.

> *"Our purpose is to please God, not people. He alone examines the motives of our hearts." 1 Thessalonians 2:4 (New Living Translation)*

We can't win and maintain the approval of God and man at the same time. We need to look for God's affirmation alone. If you've relied on people for your confidence for a long time, it may take a while to completely break the power of fear. But you will conquer it if you do not shrink from your decision.

> *"And you shall <u>do what is right and good in the sight of the Lord,</u> that it may be well with you and that you may go in and possess the good land of which the Lord swore to your fathers..." Deuteronomy 6:18*

Boldness can be defined by what we will happily do and say in front of other people. Sometimes you will need to make decisions and say things that people don't like if you want to please God.

> *"The day after the Passover, the children of Israel went out with boldness <u>in the sight of</u> all the Egyptians." Numbers 33:3*

We need to be bold and strong to wholly follow God. We need to believe that God is our protector, our provider, our promoter and our portion. He is able to meet your needs and bring His will to pass in your life.

> *"Be strong and courageous; do not be afraid nor dismayed before the king of Assyria (that person in your life who intimidates you), nor before all the multitude that is with him. With him is the arm of flesh but with us is the Lord our God <u>to help</u> us and to <u>fight our battles</u>." 2 Chronicles 32:7-8 (brackets mine)*

Make a choice today. Don't put your trust in man any more. Don't look to people for reassurance or confidence. God is the only One who is able to protect and reassure you.

"Whatever you do, do it heartily, <u>as to the Lord and not to men</u> knowing that <u>from the Lord you will receive the reward</u>." Colossians 3:23-24

Let's seek to please God alone. Let's aim to be noticed by Him and to impress Him rather than important people. Like Jesus, let's live our lives for the Lord.

"I always do those things that please Him." John 8:29b

Make David's confession your confession. "Lord, I place my trust in You alone." Dozens of times throughout the Psalms, David reiterated these words:

"In the Lord I put my trust" Psalm 11:1

It's not something we do once. It's an action we do every time we are feeling intimidated or insecure about the views of man. Trusting God is a daily, even hourly, decision. It relieves tension and lifts burdens. It reminds us who our confidence really comes from.

Prayer

Dear Lord,

Thank You for Your Word to me. I recognise that I have sought to please people. I have looked for man's approval and I am sorry. Where I have hankered after people's approval, I ask You to forgive me. (*Now be specific. Tell the Lord which person or people you have been afraid of or sought to please. Tell Him who you have been intimidated by or who you have tried to impress. Tell the Lord that you are sorry.)*

I renounce all fear of man. Fear is not my portion! I have not been given fear by God. I take authority over the spirit of fear and I dispel all fear in Jesus's name. I rebuke fear from every area of my life and from every relationship. I will not live in fear or under fear any more. God has given me power, love and sound thinking instead! Hallelujah!

I want to please You, O Lord, and You alone. I will no longer seek first to make people happy. I will now seek first to make You happy. I am now a God-pleaser!

I put my trust in You today. I look to You to meet all my emotional and physical needs.

In Jesus's name,

Amen.

Daily confessions to help you put your confidence in Christ

You might find it useful to confess these Bible verses over your life. Personalise them so that instead of saying, "The Lord shall be your confidence," you confess in prayer, "The Lord is my confidence!"

"For the Lord shall be your confidence, firm and strong." Proverbs 3:26 (Amplified)

"Trusting the Lord means safety." Proverbs 29:25 (New Living Translation)

"I always do those things that please Him." John 8:29b

"In the Lord, I put my trust..." Psalm 11:1

PS

It's amazing how often we tolerate fear. I've heard strong people talk about fear of heights, spiders, rats, insects, public speaking, driving in cities, driving on highways, and so on.

This chapter has focused on the fear of man, but I encourage you to see all fear as an enemy and to seek to overcome it in every area. When God delivered me from fear, I realised that I was still afraid of one thing: horses! I like to go for long runs in the countryside and the route I usually took had a new set of visitors – some huge four-legged friends!

For a few days, I avoided the offending field. Then one day, I thought to myself, "Why am I tolerating fear?" It was easy to argue quite reasonably about this one – horses are much bigger than me and I'm sure there must be stories of deaths by trampling. But I had made a stand against fear and I didn't want it to occupy any area of my life. So as I jumped over a small wall and into the field full of horses, I declared, "Spirit of fear, I rebuke you in Jesus's name!" and I ran past the horses. I got through the field and rejoiced in my new victory.

Now I had to go back the same way to return home! As I did so, there was a new peace. I said, "Jesus, I am safe because you are my shield." I ran through that field again and for the first time in my adult life, I had no fear of horses. All I had to do was take up my authority in Christ and resist. I encourage you to do the same. The freedom you will enjoy in the end will be well worth the fight!

Chapter 4

Special

I became a Christian as a teenager and I had a strong sense that God's hand was upon me. I read the Bible from start to finish by the time I was fifteen and at sixteen I received a word that I was destined for leadership. Sadly, I backslid as a student, but I rededicated my life to Jesus in my early twenties. Within a matter of months, I gave up a promising career for a part-time job that would pay my way through Bible college. I was zealous for God and worked hard to get back to the place where I belonged. I rose early to pray and study. I was out on the streets every Saturday to share the gospel. Whenever the church doors were open for a meeting, I was there. I was hungry, in love with the Lord and eager to grow.

Soon I started to receive public prophecies about my life and ministry. One time, a close friend walked into church while a pastor was prophesying over someone and she thought, "That must be Jo." She was right. God was confirming His call on my life. One week, three different people gave me words that I was special to God and that He had a great purpose for my life. Those words went deep into my heart. The problem was that on the way down, they got twisted.

The prophecies made me feel important and made me think that I was special. Let me explain something crucial. You are very special to God and so am I. But what makes you and I special is not the call of God on our lives. It's not our gifting or talent. It's not our ministry or achievements. I am special because I am a daughter of my heavenly Father. You and I are special because we belong to Jesus.

I didn't know all that back then so I started to think that I was more important than other people. That was a problem. When God calls us to ministry, He calls us to lay down our lives for His people. He calls us to be servants. He called me because He values you.

On one hand, I was insecure and fragile, but on the other, I had an inflated view of myself. Insecurity and pride are a particularly unpleasant mix. In fact, insecurity is all too often the root of pride. But irrespective of the root, if we think more highly of ourselves than we ought, we are on dangerous ground. The Bible gives us a list of things that God hates, that are an abomination to Him. Guess what is right at the top of that list?

"A proud look (the spirit that makes one overestimate himself and underestimate others)..." Proverbs 6:17 (Amplified)

It's an attitude of heart that can be summed up in one look, one reaction or comment. "Who does she think she is?" "Why on earth would they choose him (rather than me)?" Satan fell because he started to think he was something special. The irony is that he was a highly valued angel before the position went to his head.

He was thrown out of heaven for overestimating himself. Jesus is a servant king. He won't tolerate those who think that they are better than other people and lord themselves over fellow believers. Because the devil lost his position to pride, he constantly seeks to sow pride into the hearts of God's people.

The Message Bible talks about "eyes that are arrogant" in this verse. When we look down on other people, when we think that their opinions are less valuable than ours, when we belittle the gifting or experience of brothers or sisters, we place ourselves outside the favour and blessing of God:

> *"He who has a haughty look and a proud and arrogant heart, I cannot and I will not tolerate." Psalm 101:5b (Amplified)*

Have you rolled your eyes at someone else's unimpressive performance or behaviour? Have you questioned the decisions of God or your leaders when they appoint others to positions you thought you should fill?

> *"There is a class of people – oh how lofty are their eyes and their raised eyelids." Proverbs 30:13*

Maybe you have shaken your head at the way a brother has made the same mistakes again and again. Perhaps it gives you a kick to put down the people around you. It may start out as an innocent thing, but without a check, it can get out of control. You may have unwittingly made a sport out of undermining your wife and now even your children have started to follow suit. Perhaps you have got into the habit of patronising a member of your team. Maybe you regularly criticise a certain colleague or friend. It might be harsh reactions, cutting remarks, the roll of an eye, an impatient answer or a knowing look.

When we develop an inflated self-image, we find it harder to see the truth. We are no longer looking with 20/20 vision and we are open to error. Sometimes we also separate ourselves from others:

> *"The pride of your heart has deceived you, you who dwell in the hidden places of the rock." Obadiah 1:3*

John warned believers in his third letter about a man called Diotrephes:

> *"He loves to have the pre-eminence among the church but he does not receive us." 3 John 9*

When pride takes root, we want to look good. We want to be respected and honoured with a position and a title. We may even close our ears to the wisdom and guidance of men and women of God, just as Diotrephes did. When we think too highly of our own gifting and talents, we are in danger of driving away the One who gave us our gifts.

> *"No one who is conceited will be my friend." Psalm 101:5 (Contemporary English Version)*

Conceit is when we have an excessively favourable opinion of ourselves. We build ourselves up in our own eyes and believe our own propaganda. It's time to face the truth because as long as we overestimate ourselves, it will limit how God can use us.

"Do you see a man wise in his own eyes, there is more hope for a fool than for him." **Proverbs 26:12**

When we are conceited, we see brothers or sisters lead or teach and think we could do it better. We watch colleagues make mistakes and assume we would be a good replacement. We don't know the hearts of others and we need to be careful not to believe our own report rather than the truth.

"He flatters himself in his own eyes." **Psalm 36:2**

Out of love, God will often wait until we have dealt with conceit before He will lift us up. So with the convicting help of the Holy Spirit, let's search our hearts to see what's there.

The symptoms of pride

The Bible helps us work out what's in our hearts. Because we know the symptoms of chickenpox, we can get a proper diagnosis and a doctor can prescribe the right treatment. In the same way, God's Word explains some of the symptoms of pride so that we can identify it and deal with the problem.

As you read, I encourage you to ask God to reveal the contents of your soul. Once an issue is exposed to the light and we accept the truth, we can find freedom and fulfilment. These are some of the symptoms:

Quarrels. When someone makes a statement, I present an opposing argument. I challenge people about their choices, leadership or authority. I believe that what I have to say is very important and that others should listen. "Proud people have a fondness for controversy and disputes and strife about words which result in... quarrels and... suspicion." 1 Timothy 6:4 "Pride only breeds quarrels." Proverbs 13:10

Contentions. Everything is a contest. I compete with friends and colleagues for position or attention. I might not always let it show, but I feel it within. Certain people easily antagonise me. I strive to be heard, to make my point and to influence others. "By pride and insolence only comes contention and strife." Proverbs 13:10 (Amplified)

Impatience. My time and my goals are more important than the time and goals of those around me. People sometimes tell me that I'm direct or abrupt, perhaps even harsh. "The patient in spirit is better than the proud in spirit." Ecclesiastes 7:8

Christianity is a democracy. I find it difficult to accept authority when I'm not the one exercising it. I feel I have the right to have my say and influence decisions. I believe that God speaks to and through me just as much as He speaks through leaders. Motivated by pride, Miriam and Aaron challenged Moses's lifestyle and leadership. "Has the Lord indeed spoken only through Moses? Has He not spoken through us also?" Numbers 12:2

Shame. I believe I should be given responsibility and position. But if it's withheld, I feel let down and ashamed. Jesus told the parable of the dinner party. Certain guests thought they deserved the best seats. They tried to secure their positions but were asked to move. That's embarrassing. "When pride comes then comes shame." Proverbs 11:2

Aloofness. I keep a distance from people. I prefer to keep myself to myself; I don't feel like one of the crowd. I enjoy my privacy. I take advice when it concurs with my opinion but quickly reject challenging views. "He who separates himself and estranges himself seeks his own desire; he breaks out against wise and sound judgment." Proverbs 18:1 (Amplified)

I'm always right. My father used to respond to arguments with the statement, 'You were right, you're always right and this time you are right!' It's all too easy to be convinced by my own PR and to think that I'm more likely than others to know what's best. "In the pride of your heart you say I am a god, I sit on the throne... but you are a man." Ezekiel 28:2

The problem with pride

Pride is one of the most dangerous diseases of the human heart. It is one of the few attitudes that repel God. Whereas insecurity, jealousy or defensiveness are self-destructive, pride actually causes God to resist us. It's no good trying to resist the devil if God is resisting you. God only backs us when we are humble:

> *"God resists the proud but gives grace (favour) to the humble. Therefore submit to God. Resist the devil and he will flee from you." James 4:6-7*

When I overestimate myself, when I look down on someone else's abilities, when I roll my eyes at the behaviour of another - God will keep me at a distance until I humble myself. I want God to work with me and not against me. I need His help, His love and His favour in my life so I need to learn to be humble:

> *"And whoever exalts himself will be humbled and he who humbles himself will be exalted." Matthew 23:12*

It's not just that God dislikes pride. The Bible tells us that He won't put up with it:

> *"He who has a haughty look and a proud and arrogant heart, I cannot and I will not tolerate." Psalm 101:5b (Amplified)*

When King Nebuchadnezzar was proud, God removed him from the throne and stripped him of his dignity and glory. Pride is a destiny destroyer.

> *"But when his heart was lifted up and his mind and spirit were hardened so that he dealt proudly, he was deposed from his kingly throne and his glory was taken from him." Daniel 5:20*

Pride also produces a hard heart and when we are hard-hearted, we alienate ourselves from God. He is looking for those who are humble and soft-hearted. When we think too highly of ourselves, we can become blinkered or blinded to the truth. We don't want to hear the perspectives of others, unless they are from those whom we particularly respect. Even then, a proud heart will pick and choose what it accepts. Pride makes us dismiss people with less experience, fewer years or less gifting.

"The pride of your heart has deceived you." Jeremiah 49:16

If God won't tolerate pride then I don't want to tolerate it either. The former mayor of New York, Rudolph Giuliani, declared war on crime in his city. He instructed the police to show zero tolerance towards offenders. Every offence, however small or insignificant, was punished. Law and order was re-established in New York and crime levels plummeted. I think that's the kind of attitude we need to develop towards pride. Declare war on it!

But why?

Pride is a deep-rooted enemy within and the devil takes every chance to tempt us. We all have to resist the desire to be proud. However, at times pride is the result of something beneath the surface. When that's the case, it's important to understand why we are feeling proud. If we don't deal with the root cause, it will be harder to stay free from the sin. If we detect what this is, it will be much easier to put things right for the long run.

Insecurity

If people put you down as you were growing up or undermined your self-confidence in adult life, you may have reacted by separating yourself from the crowd. You push the world away. Rather than becoming vulnerable and facing potential rejection, you protect yourself and take every compliment and endorsement to heart as evidence of your value. You end up believing that you're important and expect respect. Sometimes you keep people at a distance and project an image of self-sufficiency. That's never the answer:

"In his self-sufficiency, he will be in distress." Job 20:22

If you grew up in a family where knowledge was king, you may have learned to use what you know to make you feel important. Rather than facing your insecurity, you build yourself up in your own imagination and convince yourself that you are more able than the people around you. That way, you don't have to contemplate the awful truth that others might be happier or more gifted than you. You unwittingly decide that you don't need anyone's help to succeed. You give an appearance of self-confidence and stand slightly aloof from the crowd. You regularly comment on church or family issues rather than opening up about your own problems. You won't allow the views of others to reach your heart, partly because their comments may threaten your self-belief. But you don't let them know that. In fact, you may not even realise it yourself. The Bible says in Jeremiah 17:9 that the heart is deceptive and can lie. This is a good example of when our hearts deceive us.

You believe your own propaganda that all is well, even though you know it isn't. The emotional isolation keeps you protected from threats, but creates a breeding ground for pride. You keep at a safe distance the very people God wants to use to help you. You rarely talk about the deep issues of your heart and you probably don't often acknowledge them yourself. You dismiss people's opinions and keep yourself detached from the wisdom of others. You often have a point to make or a view to air and you prefer to listen to your own conclusions than anyone else's. Insecurity may be the root, but we have to recognise that for some of us, pride is the fruit.

Success

It might be easy to be humble when we are weak and not achieving anything. As God strengthens us and promotes us, if we are not careful, we can believe that our own gifts and talents have made us powerful (Deuteronomy 8:16-18). When I start to think that my own brilliance has made me great, I am in trouble. When I start to believe that I am something special, I am on sinking sand. The Bible says that as long as King Uzziah (one of the more righteous kings of Judah) sought the Lord, God made him prosper. However, when he started to believe that he was the reason for his success and became proud and presumptuous, God removed him from the throne.

"But after Uzziah became powerful, his pride led to his downfall." 2 Chronicles 26:16 (New Living Translation)

I'm rolling in it

The Bible says that God is delighted when we prosper (Psalm 35:27b). He loves to see His children do well; it blesses His heart. All the silver and gold belong to God and He is the One who gives us the power to get wealth (Deuteronomy 8:18). The problem arises when we think we've done well because we are clever. It is never clever to be proud. It ultimately results in our destruction.

"Then you say in your heart, 'My power and the might of my hand have gained me this wealth.'" Deuteronomy 8:17.

"Your heart is lifted up because of your riches." Ezekiel 28:5b.

The Lord gives us the antidote: to focus our efforts on being rich in good works. When we see need around us and ask God to make us the answer, it helps to keep us humble in our own sight.

> *"As for the rich in this world, charge them not to be proud and arrogant and contemptuous of others, nor to set their hopes on uncertain riches, but on God, who richly and ceaselessly provides us with everything for [our] enjoyment. [Charge them] to do good, to be rich in good works, to be liberal and generous of heart, ready to share." 1 Timothy 6:17-18 (Amplified)*

Great people make mistakes

Hezekiah was one of the most loyal kings of Judah. He was zealous for the things of God. He loved to worship and make sacrifices before the Lord. He led the people back to their faith and reformed Judah in his day. God described Hezekiah as a man who did what was "good and right and true before the Lord" (2 Chronicles 31:20). He was a great example of love and purity. Yet even Hezekiah became proud when he became famous. He forgot where God had brought him from and became impressed with his own success.

> *"And many brought presents to King Hezekiah so that he was exalted in the sight of all nations. In those days*

Hezekiah was sick... But Hezekiah did not repay according to the favour shown him, for his heart was lifted up; therefore wrath was looming... Then Hezekiah humbled himself for the pride of his heart..." 2 Chronicles 32:23-26

You don't have to make it big to become enamoured with your own achievements or talents. However, the higher you fly, the greater the temptation. Thank God that King Hezekiah saw his folly. The Bible says that he humbled himself and was healed of his sickness. Unfortunately, pride reared its ugly head again when Babylonian ambassadors visited Hezekiah. With great pleasure, he showed off his treasures and riches. He was saying in his heart, "Look how successful I am." As a consequence, Hezekiah lost his entire inheritance:

"'Behold the days are coming when all that is in your house and what your fathers have accumulated until this day shall be carried to Babylon: nothing shall be left,' says the Lord." 2 Kings 20:17

God wants to promote and elevate His sons and daughters. The Bible says that when the righteous rule in a city, the people rejoice. It's God's desire to raise faithful men and women up to great positions of authority and responsibility. But can you pass the pride test? Can God give you incredible gifts and victories without them going to your head? Have a think about your own view of yourself and what you would like the world to know about you. Do you tell people when you've done well? Do you broadcast your achievements among your circle of friends? Do you want people to be impressed by your successes? Maybe it's time to put some 'pride protectors' in your life.

1. Don't sing your own praises

Make a decision to leave the celebration of your success to others. Then give God the glory when they do:

> *"Let another man praise you and not your own mouth; a stranger and not your own lips." Proverbs 27:2*

If you blow your own trumpet and draw attention to yourself, people will just see you. Perhaps it's time to stop talking about your achievements and talents. When God raises you up, He is glorified. God has no role in self-promotion. That's not His way.

> *"To seek one's own glory is not glory." Proverbs 25:27*

The Bible promises that a man's gift makes room for him. You don't need to tell people what you're good at and where your gifts lie. Let God promote you. Don't do it yourself anymore. It just leads to disappointment when no one gives you the recognition you desire.

> *"<u>When people commend themselves, it doesn't count for much. The important thing is for the Lord to commend them</u>." 2 Corinthians 10:18 (New Living Translation)*

If you stop seeking man's recognition, you can receive what you really need - direct from the King of Kings. And when you no longer crave human recognition, God will know that you are ready.

2. Don't take compliments to heart

A simple lesson I have learned is this: don't take the praise of people to heart. Whenever someone congratulates you for your great singing or worship leading, don't thank them. Say, 'Praise God.' Whenever anyone is impressed by your job or your car, don't lap it up. Lift Him up instead. Tell admirers, encouragers or flatterers that it is God who has given you everything. Don't let people's praises go to your heart (or your head). Raise them all to God. Always remember to thank Him for using and choosing you. That will at least begin the process of resisting pride.

"Jesus said: 'I do not receive honour from men.'" John 5:41

Jesus would not look to people for praise or admiration. He looked to God the Father to honour Him. If words reassure you in the depths of your being then you might need to become more careful. Before you know it, disinheritance is knocking at your door.

"How do you believe, who receive honour from one another?" John 5:44

We mustn't seek to be celebrated by the words or actions of others. God is the One who crowns us with honour:

"And _You_ have crowned him (that's you and me) with glory and honour." Psalm 8:35 (words in brackets are mine)

3. You don't have anything to prove

That was one of the most liberating revelations of my life! I don't need to prove anything to anyone. I am what

I am by the favour of God (1 Corinthians 15:10). It's His job to use me, it's His job to promote me and it's His job to vindicate me. I don't have to prove anything to anyone. Knowing that will go a long way to setting you free from self-promotion. You're already a success simply because you're His. Your heart is your job. Your future is God's.

True humility

God tells us to humble ourselves. Moses, one of the greatest Old Testament leaders, was described by the Lord as very humble (Numbers 12:3). The apostle Paul, author of one third of the New Testament, said that he served the Lord with all humility (Acts 20:19). Humility is a sense of <u>moral insignificance and unselfish concern for the welfare of others</u>. It's having a self-image of being low in rank and status. Jesus said, "I am meek and humble of heart." Matthew 11:29 (New American Standard Bible)

When Daniel was brought before Nebuchadnezzar to tell the king his dream and its meaning, he was quick to give God the credit. He refused to allow the king to be impressed with his performance. He told Nebuchadnezzar that he was just God's messenger, not some extra special leader:

> *"But as for me, this secret has not been revealed to me because I have more wisdom than anyone living, but... that you may know the thoughts of your heart." Daniel 2:30*

A pastor friend always collects guest speakers from the airport himself rather than send someone else. He then becomes their chauffeur while they are with him in order to remind himself of his station. The Bible tells us to humble ourselves under the mighty hand of God. Here the word humble is a verb. It's a so-called doing word and something that we need to carry out ourselves. To humble literally means to lower or debase oneself.

Growing in humility

If you recognise pride within you, it's time to start humbling yourself. There are lots of ways that we can remind ourselves of our true status. Asking the Holy Spirit for His help is a good starting point. If you want to eradicate pride from your life, you need to deal with your mind, your mouth and your actions:

Mind. It's time to have a sober opinion of yourself. Yes, you are probably wonderfully gifted, but you are not better than other people. Paul taught that each one should "...not think more highly of himself than he ought to think, but to think soberly..." (Romans 12:3). Why not have a rethink? In fact, it's probably time to join Paul in his confession: "Christ Jesus came into the world to save sinners, of whom I am chief." I'm not suggesting you become sin-conscious, but that you remember you would be nothing without Christ. If you know that your pride is a product of insecurity, allow God to make you secure. Then climb down from that lonely hill and open up your heart and life to serve other people. If pride has been rooted in success, it's time to start (and then not stop) acknowledging who it is that has prospered your way.

Mouth. Don't talk about your latest achievement or your new job. Keep your successes to yourself. "If you have been foolish in exalting yourself... <u>put your hand on your</u> <u>mouth</u>." (Proverbs 30:32) Celebrate others instead, especially those you compete with. Use your mouth to break down your pride. I tell people about my mistakes and say sorry when I am wrong. It helps keep me humble. Tell one or two close friends that you have declared war on pride. Give them examples of how it manifests itself and ask them to point out any time when they see you behaving arrogantly. It sounds hard but it's only difficult because it requires humility. When we humble ourselves, we attract God's favour.

Motion. It's time to do what servants do. Volunteer for the tasks or jobs at church that you believe the least qualified should do. Serve a leader who you think you're better qualified or more talented than. Make the tea or coffee at work and serve the family member or friend who you previously lorded it over. Don't keep yourself to yourself.

As well as putting things right for the future, we need to come before God and ask Him to forgive us for the way we have behaved in the past. Go to God in prayer and tell Him how you have been proud. A proud heart is a hard heart. When you change your mind and your ways, God is then able to change your heart. Ask Him to take away your heart of stone and give you a heart of flesh.

David refused to allow his heart to be proud before the Lord. Scripture instructs us to humble ourselves and David clearly chose to do this:

> *"And I will be even more undignified than this, and will be humble in my own sight." 2 Samuel 6:22*

David determined that he would keep himself humble in his own eyes and he deliberately behaved in ways that would keep him human in the sight of the people. He always gave glory to God.

It amazes me that God wants to glorify you and I (Romans 8:30). He desires to exalt us and to give us prominence (1 Peter 5:5b). But He wants to do that when we aren't looking for it. When we no longer want to prove ourselves, be noticed or celebrated, He can get to work. By that time, we'll be ready to give all the glory to God.

> *"Not unto us, not unto us Oh Lord, but to Your name be given glory." Psalm 115:1*

Prayer

Dear Lord,

Thank you for Your extraordinary love and patience with me. I am sorry for the times I have been proud. I am sorry for the occasions when I've tried to attract attention to myself. I am sorry for when I've blown my own trumpet. I am sorry for being conceited and for thinking too highly of myself. I am sorry for putting others down. I am sorry for trying to prove my worth. I apologise for allowing pride to grow in the soil of an insecure heart. Please forgive me, Lord, in Your great mercy.

I choose today to humble myself. I will watch what I think, I will guard what I say and I will behave as a servant. Please help me to follow Jesus's wonderful example.

I humble myself before You and ask for Your help to keep me humble at all times.

I give You all the glory for every achievement and victory in my life.

I love You and I thank You.

In Jesus's name,

Amen.

Daily confessions to help you cultivate a humble heart

You might find it useful to confess these Bible verses over your life. Personalise them so that instead of saying, "Therefore humble yourselves under the mighty hand of God, that He may exalt you in due time," you confess in prayer, "I humble myself under Your mighty hand, Lord, knowing that You will lift me up at the right time."

"Therefore humble yourselves under the mighty hand of God, that He may exalt you in due time." 1 Peter 5:6

"When people commend themselves, it doesn't count for much. The important thing is for the Lord to commend them." 2 Corinthians 10:18 (New Living Translation)

"Not unto us, not unto us, Oh Lord, but to Your name be given glory." Psalm 114:1

"He who humbles himself will be exalted." Matthew 23:12

Chapter 5

You're meant to be my friend!

Several years ago, I ministered what I thought was an excellent message on fear. I went into the Greek and Hebrew and expounded dozens of key scriptures. I'm a preacher so preaching well is important to me. Afterwards, I had a great sense of achievement and chatted to people with satisfaction. My husband and I always give each other feedback after we minister so that we can learn and grow. When I got into the car to go home, I was sure that he would commend my message and we would praise God together.

I could not have been more wrong! "How on earth was anyone supposed to get free from fear today?" he asked as I fastened my seatbelt. "As ministers, we're supposed to equip the saints. Today, people's heads got filled, but their hearts remained the same. Those who arrived bound left the same way."

I tried for a while to defend myself, but he was right. I had preached *about* fear, yet I had not told the people how to be free *from* fear. I felt terrible.

My husband's feedback that day taught me one of the most valuable lessons I have learned in ministry. But it came with a price tag – a painful rebuke that left me reeling with disappointment.

"Reproofs of instruction are the way of life." **Proverbs 6:23**

As we saw in chapter three, the Bible sometimes uses vocabulary that isn't common in everyday conversation. As a result, we can read the words but we may miss the meaning. Let's look at what this verse is telling us.

The word 'reproof' means rebuke and 'instruction' here doesn't refer to one person explaining to another how something is done - it means correction. In fact, the New Living Translation interprets reproofs of instruction as 'corrective discipline'. This is the kind of reprimand a parent will give their child when they have misbehaved.

Believe it or not, the Bible is telling us that correction is the route to a great life. Rebukes help us understand our mistakes and change our behaviour so that we can become the people we need to be to fulfil our potential.

Most of us will have experienced correction as an adult. Perhaps your spouse has pointed out your inadequacies or a friend has exposed your secret faults. Maybe a pastor has highlighted an area for growth or a relative has revealed your weaknesses. The truth is that not many of us like having our attitudes or behaviour challenged. We don't jump up and down and celebrate! We feel under attack and defend ourselves.

If it's for my good, why am I so defensive?

When an army is under attack, it must defend itself. A fort is built to defend a city from enemy raids. So why is it that many of us react as though we are under siege when friends, colleagues, bosses, leaders, pastors or spouses speak into our lives?

If correction is one of God's ways of bringing blessing and change, of preparing us to achieve our dreams, we must ask ourselves: 'Why am I so defensive?"

I love the lesson we learn from Isaac's wife Rebekah in Genesis. She was expecting her first child, but her pregnancy wasn't going well. Perhaps she was in pain or maybe she was unduly tired, we don't know. What we do know is that Rebekah inquired of the Lord:

"If all is well then why am I like this?" Genesis 25:22

Perhaps it's time for us to ask God: "If correction is meant for my good, why do I recoil on the inside every time anyone tries to comment on my life or behaviour?" "Why do I become aggressive or critical of the person who is trying to shine a light on my ways?" There are a number of explanations that might account for our reactions.

1. Words hurt

The Bible says in Proverbs 18:21 that "Death and life are in the power of the tongue." There is a common childhood saying: "Sticks and stones may break my bones, but words will never hurt me." I wish that were true. In reality, many people have suffered as a result of unkind, unfair or hurtful words. For some, as you were growing up, parents, relatives, siblings, teachers, leaders or friends wounded you with their words.

"There is one who speaks like the piercings of a sword."
Proverbs 12:18

Words can be like arrows. They can hurt our feelings, squash our dreams and even damage our view of ourselves. These can be especially painful when they are spoken by those closest to us or in authority over us – the people we trust and love. When cruel words are spoken to children over a sustained period, the effects can be particularly devastating. They can crush even the strongest little soul.

If you've suffered verbal attacks in the past, when you hear words of correction, you may see a gun to your head. You know the tongue's power to destroy. You know that words can hurt. So at the first sign of negativity, you resist. You protect yourself against attack. If I thought someone was holding a gun to my head, I would do everything in my power to defend myself too.

We can end up thinking any corrective word is a weapon for our destruction. We therefore learn to build walls and defence mechanisms to repel what we imagine are the cruel attacks of others.

Job became defensive because of the critical words of his companions during his darkest hour. Job needed love and companionship. His so-called friends gave him advice and speculative rebukes. There is a time for feedback and there is a time for just being there for someone. When a friend is suffering, they probably don't need pointed fingers or clever answers. As a result of these untimely comments, Job retorted:

"I will defend my own ways." Job 13:15b

If you have been hurt by the words of others, it will be really important to ask God to heal your wounded heart. Come to the Lord in prayer and tell Him exactly what was said to you and how it made you feel. Pour out your heart to God and ask Him to heal you. He is the Master Restorer. As you release the pain, you will find relief.

Perhaps you have already been healed, but the experiences you have gone through have affected your outlook. Maybe it's time to allow the Word to renew your perspective.

2. Growing up in a word vacuum

Some people grow up without any correction at all. If you were denied the affirming guidance of a father or a mother when you were young, if you lacked the direction and discipline of a loving carer, you may have become overly independent. You may be uncomfortable when people try to give you uninvited support.

The Bible says in Hebrews 11:3 that the "worlds were framed by the word of God". In the same way, as we grow up, our lives are framed by the words of those who are influential around us. If those words are cruel or controlling, that will create wounds and confusion. If those words are missing altogether, we are denied the framework that we need. Like a plant growing up a trellis, so are children supported and shaped by words of authority in their lives. If you never received affirmation or correction, you will need to learn how to receive comments that are intended to build you up, encourage you and, yes, correct you.

"Train up a child in the way that he should go and when he is old, he will not depart from it." Proverbs 22:6

Parents and carers have a responsibility to train their children in love and to map out safe boundaries. This provides a growing soul with confidence and security. It can destabilise a child when that training is missing. If you realise that you lacked parental guidance and support, it will be important to go to God in prayer and ask Him to heal your heart. The Bible is the greatest love letter in history and I recommend that you go to Scripture and receive the words that God speaks over your life. You could start by meditating on Psalm 139:13-14, 1 John 3:1 and 1 Peter 2:9.

3. Relying on affirmation

There could be other reasons why you find correction difficult. Perhaps your security depends on the affirmation of others. If they are challenging rather than congratulating you, it can make you feel insecure. We looked at insecurity in chapter two so that you will know by now how to become more secure in Christ.

Rejection can make you feel extremely vulnerable. Whether it's a lifetime of rejection or just a season, it can make you understandably over-sensitive. First and foremost, it is important to open your heart and ask God to heal you. Rejection is possibly the most painful of human experiences. Tell the Lord how you suffered and how it made you feel. Ask Him to restore you.

At the same time, try to understand that the comments of others are not necessarily arrows that are intended to hurt. They may be loving suggestions to help you grow and mature into the person God destined you to be.

The problem

The word 'defend' means to set on high, out of the reach of others. When we defend ourselves, we place ourselves out of the reach of those that God has put into our lives to help us grow. In fact, all too often, we put ourselves out of the reach of God.

We are called to defend others:

"Defend the poor and the fatherless." Psalm 82:3

God describes Himself as a "Defender of widows" in Psalm 68:5. However, we are *never* instructed in Scripture to defend ourselves.

Whether you have been hurt by harsh words, grown up without instruction, placed your confidence in the views of others or suffered from rejection, it will be important to ask God to restore you. A whole, healthy person does not get edgy and anxious when they are corrected.

"All scripture is given by inspiration of God and is profitable for doctrine, for reproof, for correction, for instruction in righteousness." 2 Timothy 3:16

The Message translation of this verse says: "Scripture is God-breathed and useful one way or another - showing us truth, exposing our rebellion, correcting our mistakes and training us to live God's way. Through the word we are shaped up for the tasks God has for us."

How do we hear God's Word? Essentially, there are four ways: by reading the Bible, listening in prayer, receiving the teaching of others and through the people around us. We need to be open for God to speak to us however He chooses. The Lord often uses others to expose our rebellion, correct our mistakes and train us to live God's way. Others can see what we can't.

Change your thinking

The people around you may be just as defensive as you are, so you can't look to them as an example. We need to accept what God says and change the way we view correction.

"Do not be conformed to this world, but be transformed by the renewing of your mind..." Romans 12:2

The New Living Translation makes this verse very clear: "Don't copy the behaviour and customs of this world, but let God transform you into a new person by changing the way you think." As we start to meditate on God's perspective of correction, we will start to yearn for the change and growth that it can produce.

Wing mirrors

Since passing my driving test as a teenager, I'd owned a series of vehicles that were just for convenience and getting from A to B. But a couple of years ago, my husband decided it was time to buy me a truly beautiful car. I was blessed with a turquoise blue convertible that made me feel on top of the world when I drove it. However, a few weeks after it was delivered, I was reversing into a parking space when I heard a ghastly crunch! I had ploughed straight into another car. I couldn't believe it. I had been looking out of my back window but my rear wings obstructed my view. What did I learn from that agonising experience? I needed to use my wing mirrors!

The Bible says that we "see in a mirror dimly". In other words, what we see when we examine ourselves is not always accurate. The people around us see more. They have a three hundred and sixty degree perspective. The people in my life are like my wing mirrors. They see what I can't. Unless I listen to them and understand what they are saying, I will be in danger of crashing my way through life. I will probably offend and hurt others without even realising it.

One of the reasons why the enemy makes it so tempting to resist correction is that we are the ones who suffer when we close up.

> *"How I have hated instruction and my heart despised correction. I have not obeyed the voice of my teachers, nor inclined my ear to those who instructed. I was on the verge of total ruin..." Proverbs 5:12-14*

When we cannot receive instruction, we are hurting ourselves and cutting off a channel of God's blessing:

"He who <u>disdains instruction despises his own soul,</u> but he who heeds rebuke gets understanding." Proverbs 15:32

People say that you can't change others, but you can change yourself. If that's true then it might be a good idea to find out what can be changed about you so that you can become a better, more loving person and more useful to God. My husband is committed to seeing me fulfil my potential so he constantly offers feedback and correction. I love it when he tells me how well I've done! But I definitely grow more when he tells me what I could do differently next time to be more effective. Like medicine, correction doesn't taste nice, but it does me good. Any loving parents will discipline their sons and daughters. So if we're children of the Most High, we should expect correction because we're loved.

"As you endure this divine discipline, remember that God is treating you as his own children... <u>No discipline is enjoyable while it is happening—it's painful!</u> But <u>afterwards</u> there will be a peaceful harvest of <u>right living</u> for those who are trained in this way." Hebrews 12:7,11 (New Living Translation)

The correction of others is our chance to find out how we can live life in a way that will please God and bless others. It is often God's way of training and shaping us. It will help us achieve our dreams.

But what about you?

There have been countless times when my husband has tried to point something out in my life and

I have immediately tried to shift the focus from my shortcomings to his. He might be challenging me about my moods so I confront him about the last time he was mean! It's just another way of avoiding facing the issue that has been raised. It's a way of saying, "I'm not so bad. You have issues too!"

When we want to grow and fulfil our potential, we must learn to accept feedback. We must stop changing the subject, avoiding the issue or deflecting attention from our problem by mentioning others' flaws. Jesus put it this way:

> *"Why do you look at the speck in your brother's eye, but do not consider the plank in your own eye?" Matthew 7:3*

When I'm the topic of conversation, that's not the time for me to try and talk about another person's mistakes. We need to be the focus until we've acknowledged what's being said and digested what it means for our lives. It's better to choose another day to raise the problems with your partner or friend.

Don't blame me!

If we don't deflect attention from our issues then we often blame someone for them. It all started at the very beginning. No sooner had sin entered the world than blame appeared. The first thing that Adam did when God confronted him about his mistake was to blame his wife. Not much has changed in many families and relationships since! I've had to work hard on this in my life. We all seem to want to blame someone for our mistakes! A colleague asks you why you are being so grumpy and, rather than judging yourself, you blame the way your boss treated you. You shout at the children. Instead of acknowledging your wrongdoing, you blame their behaviour for your outburst.

You and I are always responsible for our own attitudes and actions. We will always have an excuse, but the Bible says that love is not easily provoked. If I snap or shout, if I am late or unreliable, if I get drunk or commit adultery, I am responsible. I cannot blame the provocative behaviour of someone else.

When we stop blaming and start taking responsibility for our actions, God can work on us and change us into His likeness. When we blame others, we are covering up our mistakes and staying in the darkness.

Correction is key

The Bible is very clear about the importance of receiving correction. It even says that if we refuse to be corrected then we are stupid!

> *"Whoever loves instruction loves knowledge but he who hates correction is stupid."* Proverbs 12:1

Scripture links our prosperity and success with the ability to be 'put right' by others.

> *"Poverty and shame will come to him who disdains correction."* Proverbs 13:18

Many businesspeople pride themselves on their attention to feedback. The chief executive of a hugely successful British restaurant chain once said, "I am only as good as the last meal I served." He was saying that customer feedback was essential to his success. It's the same in our lives. If we can learn to listen to God's voice through others, we will grow.

A while back, I was eating dinner with family and friends. During the meal, my nine year old daughter questioned me out of the blue. "Mummy, why do you always eat with your mouth open?" This was then followed by an exaggerated impersonation of how I ate. As you can imagine, I was horrified and responded quickly. "Abigail, don't be rude! Of course I don't eat with my mouth open... do I, daddy?" (Remember we had guests with us). I was shocked at my husband's response. "I gave up trying to stop you eating with your mouth open about fifteen years ago. Sometimes I turn up the music to drown out the noise!"

I was appalled. I started to think about all the different places where I had eaten and all the people I had dined with: family, friends, members of the congregation, pastors, colleagues - the list went on. For a while, I protested. However, in the end I had to concede defeat. I decided to work on this ugly, lifelong habit. It was excruciating to have something so embarrassing pointed out by my child in a room full of guests, but it was well worth it. In just two weeks, I cracked the problem. As a result of the brutal honesty of my nine year old daughter, I am now a more sociable eater!

We never know who will expose our weaknesses, character flaws, annoying habits or unkindness. But if we listen out for God's corrective voice, we can be changed for the better.

Want to be your best?

How hungry are you to be more like Jesus? How much do you want to grow into the man or woman that God intends you to be? The keener we are to grow and to become our best, the more we need to hear and heed correction from those around us.

There was a period when our church was working closely with more experienced pastors from another church. I told those pastors that I was hungry to grow in God and that I wanted them to feel free to correct me at any time and in front of anyone. I had decided that my enthusiasm for God was greater than my need for dignity.

"To a hungry soul, every bitter thing is sweet." Proverbs 27:7b

This means that a hungry disciple would rather swallow unpleasant correction, however bitter it may taste, than stay the same way. The desire to be God's best becomes greater than the need for self-preservation.

God put a certain woman in my life for a season of growth. She was incredibly perceptive and possessed great authority. She would correct me, sometimes on a weekly basis. One week she picked up a hint of jealousy towards my friend. Another week, it was insecurity. Some time later, she detected a grasping attitude. Every time she exposed my issues, it was in a room full of people. And I kept going back for more! I thank God for that season. I'm not saying it was easy, but I am grateful to God that He showed me the state of my heart so that I could change.

"A scoffer does not love the one who corrects him nor will he go to the wise." Proverbs 15:12

We need to learn to appreciate those whom God uses to expose our shortcomings. We should draw near to people who correct us. If you avoid individuals who will challenge you, ask yourself why and try instead to get close to them. The Bible calls this wisdom. Scripture says that you can identify wisdom in a person by their willingness to accept correction.

"A fool despises his father's instruction, but <u>he who receives correction is prudent.</u>" Proverbs 15:5

Make a decision today not to shun people who challenge you. Of course there is a difference between loving correction and critical accusation. I'm not suggesting that you should subject yourself to cruel and unkind attacks. However, when God puts people in our lives who will speak the truth in love, it's prudent to embrace the corrective voice of God through them. Determine to be humble and hungry enough to receive feedback – to take the rough with the smooth.

Take it on the chin

A while back, I became acutely aware that I was being impatient with my children. I was getting irritated and frustrated far too easily and I wanted to become more patient. I know others see what I don't see so I asked a friend what she thought was my problem.

"Selfishness," was her immediate response. Selfishness? I was expecting that she might point out how busy I was or that I needed to slow down. "What do you mean?" She went on to say that lack of patience is always a lack of love because love is patient (1 Corinthians 13:4). I was more concerned with my agenda than in giving myself to them. That was a painful lesson, but it was helpful. I have worked very hard in that area for a long time. Although I'm not there yet, I'm learning to be unselfish in my relationships.

"Faithful are the wounds of a friend." Proverbs 27:6

When we allow our closest companions to speak into our lives, we will find out how we need to change. At first, it can be hard, but sooner or later you will get used to handling constructive criticism or difficult feedback.

"A wise son heeds instruction, but a scoffer does not listen to rebuke." Proverbs 13:1

If you will receive correction, God says you are wise: "He who heeds counsel is wise." (Proverbs 12:15). A scoffer is a fool or a mocker. When we listen to a rebuke, we make sure we aren't fools in the eyes of God.

However, when we deflect criticism, blame others or defend ourselves too much, the people around us will stop speaking into our lives.

"So these three men ceased answering Job because he was righteous in his own eyes." Job 32:1

As a pastor, I'm far more likely to challenge people who are capable of receiving a rebuke than those who will argue with one. We all need truth and correction, but only some of us get it.

"Obey those who rule over you, and be submissive, for <u>they watch out for your souls</u>, as those who must give account. <u>Let them do so with joy</u> and not with grief, for that would be unprofitable for you." Hebrews 13:17

When we choose to receive from those whom God has placed in our lives we will start to be moulded into the image of God.

Handling hard feedback

I know that sinking feeling when somebody questions your best efforts. When we do something with all our hearts and give it everything, it's too easy to take criticism personally.

I had an art teacher at school who tore up a picture I painted. Since becoming a pastor, I have developed the view that pastoring is a bit like painting. You pour your life into other people just as an artist pours all that they have on to a canvas. When people say they don't like what you've done, it's all too easy to think that they don't like *you*. We have to learn to separate the two things. When my teacher ripped up my picture, she was rubbishing my painting, not me.

The truth is that we will always learn more from negative than positive feedback. Even if the person criticising us or our work *is* antagonistic, there is still a genuine opportunity for us to learn. If we can separate the tone and the animosity from the words, we will be able to see if there is any truth in the assessment. You may find that some of your greatest teachers dislike you!

If we want God's best for our lives, if we want to grow into His likeness, if we want to fulfil our dreams, we will have to embrace correction. Being aware of your reactions is the first step towards responding the right way. The desire to fulfil my destiny makes me swallow difficult feedback, however painful. The only way we can change our ways is to do it wholeheartedly. Embrace every word of correction that comes your way and become someone who is easy to challenge. You will grow fast.

Prayer

Father God,

I find correction difficult. I have responded to rebukes as though I was under attack. I have not always seen correction as an opportunity for blessing.

I ask You to heal my heart where I have been wounded by words in the past. The things people have said have hurt me (*tell the Lord exactly what was said to you and how it made you feel. If you never knew the loving guidance of carers when you were growing up, ask Him to restore your soul.*) I realise that I am over-sensitive because of the experiences of the past. I ask You to renew my mind and help me to change the way I think.

I don't want to resist feedback. I want to be wise. Where I have shifted the spotlight from my problems to the problems of others, I'm sorry, Lord. Where I have blamed people and circumstances for my attitudes and behaviour, I repent, Lord.

I want to be changed to be more like You, Jesus. I want to fulfil my destiny, so have Your way in my life.

From now on, I will receive correction.

In Jesus's name,

Amen.

Daily confessions to help you become an easy person to correct

You might find it useful to confess these Bible verses over your life. Personalise them so that instead of saying, "He who heeds rebuke gets understanding," you confess in prayer, "I choose to listen to and accept rebuke so I will grow in understanding."

"He who heeds rebuke gets understanding." Proverbs 15:32

"He who has ears to hear, let him hear!" Luke 13:45

"So see to it that you do not reject Him or refuse to listen to and heed Him Who is speaking [to you now]." Hebrews 12:25 (Amplified)

"No discipline is enjoyable while it is happening—it's painful! But afterward there will be a peaceful harvest." Hebrews 12:11 (New Living Translation)

Chapter 6

Are you determined or just plain stubborn?

Stubborn means to be fixed or set in purpose or opinion; to be resolute; hard, tough or stiff. It also means to be difficult to shape or mould, like stone or wood.

Some of these adjectives are exceptionally positive. Jesus set His face like flint towards the cross. He was determined to fulfil His mission, no matter how painful the process. People who are relentless in their efforts to achieve their goals usually succeed. We must be resolute in our relationship with God or the enemy will easily lead us astray.

There are words that the dictionary says are similar in meaning: adamant, intent, steadfast, tenacious and unshakeable. So far, so good. But the list continues: intractable, rigid, inflexible, wilful and opinionated. Then the words become more negative: self-willed, cantankerous, pigheaded, rebellious, stiff-necked and unbending.

Not long after we got married, my husband and I decorated our new flat. He was better at DIY than me so he gave me the menial jobs like tea-making and vacuuming up his messes. I was fed up with being the dogsbody so I dug my heels in. I started to argue that I was adept at any task and could do half the 'real' work.

I hardened my heart each time my husband sent me on an inane errand. Why should I be his slave? In the end, I exclaimed, "I can do DIY!" With an intensely annoying expression of disbelief plastered across his face, my husband handed me a screwdriver and told me, "Change the living room door handle."

"That's easy," I muttered as I set to work. I removed each screw and, feeling wonderfully smug, pulled the handle out. I closed the door to shut out my husband's patronising guidance. I stooped down to collect the new knob to start the second part of the job. Then it dawned on me. You need an open door to fix a handle. But I'd removed the handle and shut the door! I was covered in sweat and locked in our living room.

I hollered through the door whilst my husband amused himself by leaving me there to reflect upon my stupidity for twenty minutes. What a berk! It's amazing how silly we can be when we're stubborn.

This is a harmless example, but the attitudes of our heart can get us into trouble. However easygoing you are, there are probably moments when you are stubborn. We all want our own way from time to time. For some, though, this is a bigger issue and you may see a picture of yourself painted in the pages of this chapter. I believe that if you ask God to change you, you will encounter a fresh touch of the Holy Spirit and see Him move in new ways in your life.

To fulfil our destiny, we must be determined and disciplined. The key is to remain unshakeable whilst becoming bendable. We need to grow what's good whilst breaking what's bad.

Are you stubborn?

If you're stubborn, you will sometimes find it difficult to see your own error. You will argue your point and stand firm in your own opinion. People close to you might become frustrated because you fight your corner until they surrender (whether you are right or wrong!). In effect, we harden our hearts to the views or voices of others and to hell with the consequences.

How do we harden our hearts?

You may argue your point with increasing doggedness, using reason upon reason to reject a challenge or suggestion. Others will simply switch off. You smile and nod, but inside you have rejected the words of your friend. In some cases, you make a mental note not to trust that person anymore.

When we harden our hearts, we are turning down the volume of the voices of others. We dismiss their words without stopping to search our hearts. We may even discredit the authority or validity of the messenger — gathering reasons why they are uninformed, immature or unreliable. All these are ways in which we shut our minds and our hearts to the views of others.

When we harden our hearts, we withstand convicting truth. We probably believe that we are obeying God, but very often He sends us a message through other people. We have to learn to listen with an open mind to the perspectives of others. We have to stop arguing. It might be the Spirit speaking.

"He who hardens his heart will fall." Proverbs 28:14b

When we resist the truth, we set ourselves up to fail. God has an awesome plan for your life. He has great places He wants to take you and great people He wants to release into your life as friends or mentors. However, He may have to wait until you are ready. You might be wondering why you're encountering so many delays. Look within and see if God is waiting for you to get your heart right. I don't want to scupper anything the Lord has for me because my heart is hard. I'm sure you don't want to miss out either.

We all know what it feels like to resist challenge and insist that we're right. We have to learn to stop arguing, humble ourselves and listen.

"Today if you will hear His voice, do not harden your hearts." Psalm 95:7-8, Hebrews 3:7, Hebrews 3:15, Hebrews 4:7

When your inner voice rejects the challenge of others, why not try to quieten it and hear the comments of your neighbour instead? Even if it takes all your will, choose to listen and then to accept. It demands humility, but it's worth it.

"Do not be stiff necked as your fathers were but yield yourself to the Lord... and serve..." 2 Chronicles 30:8

The New Living Translations says, "Do not be stubborn as they were but submit!" You and I need to learn to give in, to yield and to submit.

With hands lifted up, we all sing at the top of our voices, "I surrender all, I surrender all." But in reality, we only really give up what we want to. That's not surrender at all - it's self-will disguised as good religion. God teaches me to submit and yield to Him through my husband. Every time I don't get my own way, every time he puts the kibosh on my perfectly crafted plans, I learn to surrender. God doesn't show up in the flesh in my office on Monday or in my dining room on a Saturday to test my heart. He just sends my husband! When he challenges me, makes unreasonable requests or presses the wrong buttons, I discover how yielded I really am. A prophet once told my husband, "Be really tough on your wife. God is using you to prepare her for great things." My fleshly nature hates it, but by God's grace, I'm growing.

The downfall of a great man

After restoring the temple to its former glory, leading the people of Israel back to the Lord and after loving and honouring God all his life, King Josiah cut his life short. He was a wonderful leader with a great heart, but he was stubborn. The King of Eqypt attacked a neighbouring province and Josiah insisted on fighting with his neighbour against Egypt. The King of Egypt told him to relent. Josiah would not listen:

"Nevertheless Josiah would not turn his face from him but disguised himself so that he might fight with him and did not heed the words of Necho from the mouth of God."
2 Chronicles 35:22

Josiah died aged thirty nine in a battle that God did not want him to fight. We need to be careful to follow the voice of God. There are some battles that your flesh might like to fight, but if God is not leading you, it could be a distraction from His purposes. Josiah's destiny was aborted because he wouldn't listen when God was speaking through an unlikely channel. His sons (and the heirs to the throne) were not ready to rule because their hearts were not right with God so the entire nation suffered as a result of Josiah's strong self-will.

"But they refused to heed, shrugged their shoulders and stopped their ears so that they could not hear. Yes they made their hearts like flint." Zechariah 7:11-12

I know how it goes in my life. I believe I've heard God, I'm sure I'm doing the right thing and then someone challenges me. Many years ago, I ministered monthly at a cross-denominational women's group. It was growing and lives were being changed. The lady running it asked me to take over. I loved the meetings and we'd seen great fruit so I accepted with delight. I shared with a close friend who said she was not convinced that God was leading me to do that. I argued with her and gave all sorts of reasons why I was right to take the helm. In the end, the convicting power of God arrested me and I relented. I wanted to lead, but God hadn't instructed me. In fact, He was quiet on the issue, wondering why I was running around organising something that He hadn't asked me to plan. It's easy to think we're right because we want to be right.

What is it that you want to do that God has not called you to do? The protection of the Lord surrounds us <u>when</u> we are in the centre of his will.

> *"And the Lord went before them by day in a pillar of cloud to lead the way, and by night in a pillar of fire to give them light, so as to go by day and night." Exodus 13:21*

When they followed the pillar, the people of Israel were in the will of God and God protected them from their enemies:

> *"And the Angel of God, who went before the camp of Israel, moved and went behind them; and <u>the pillar of cloud went from before them and stood behind them</u>. So it came between the camp of the Egyptians and the camp of Israel." Exodus 14:19-20*

However, when we step out of His plans, we may be on our own. After Josiah's death, no king of Judah followed God. The people of Israel were soon captured by the Babylonians and taken as servants to a foreign land.

Remember that Josiah thought that he was right because it felt right. After all, God had backed him in many past battles and given him great victories. Just because you have a desire to do something does not mean that it's the right thing to do. Josiah didn't want to listen to the voice of God because He was speaking through an enemy of Israel. He didn't want to hear because he wanted his own way. This was one of Israel's greatest weaknesses and I doubt today's church is much different.

> *"Nevertheless they <u>would not hear, but stiffened their</u> <u>necks,</u> like the necks of the fathers, who did not believe... and they rejected His statutes..." 2 Kings 17:14-15*

When we refuse guidance because we dismiss the people God is speaking through, we may be rejecting God.

Why should I do that?

In the first chapter of Esther, Queen Vashti tasted the bitter fruit of stubbornness. What was her mistake? She simply refused to do what her husband asked. The King was celebrating in style with the men and, in like manner, Queen Vashti organised a party for the ladies. They were probably having a great time when the order came that she should appear before the King so he and his guests could admire her beauty. Perhaps it sounded like a bit of a drag. Maybe she felt that it was a demeaning request. We don't know why, but we do know that she said no to the King. I can imagine that the ladies were gobsmacked. No one had ever refused the King before.

Stubbornness doesn't feel like a terrible sin, but the consequences for Vashti were devastating. She lost her position, her throne, her reputation and her marriage. The more we want to do for the Lord, the more vital it is that we deal with self-will. We need to stamp out stubbornness before it steals our destiny.

How often do we feel irritated by what we're asked to do by those in authority? Perhaps a boss is being unreasonable or a leader is taking liberties. Of course, I'm not talking about abusive situations. We should never put up with any form of sexual, physical or emotional abuse. But when your husband, teacher, boss or pastor asks you to do something, how do you react? Stubbornness is an issue of the heart and not just behaviour. So how is your heart when you are called upon at an inconvenient moment?

Queen Vashti thought she was equal to the King. She didn't appreciate being told what to do and when to do it. It doesn't matter who you are or what you do, there needs to be a willingness to submit to the people God puts in your life. My husband is the senior pastor of our church. However, when he occasionally plays the drums, he is submitted to the worship leader's authority. He may sense the leading of the Spirit in a certain direction, but if the worship leader asks him to speed up or slow down, he will follow their direction with a willing heart.

How easy is it for people in authority to ask you to do something you don't want to do? Perhaps it's a job you think someone with less experience or less gifting should do. Do you respond quickly with a smile or do you balk inside? We can always hear our own stubbornness if we listen closely enough. The words may never leave our lips, but they echo inside our souls. "You've got to be kidding!" "Can't you ask someone else?" "Can't you see that I'm busy?" Sometimes we don't mind letting our self-will straight out, using a spiritual excuse: "No. That's not the way the Spirit is leading me."

God expects us to do what we're told, however powerful or gifted we may be. That's one of the ways we find out if we have a servant heart. Our head of prayer at church has an incredible attitude. He is called to lead intercession and warfare and does that faithfully. But there is nothing that he would consider beneath him. If I asked him to join the worship team, he might laugh. But he would pick up a microphone and sing. His willingness to do whatever is requested never distracts him from his mission and calling. He is a servant.

In contrast to Vashti, her successor Esther was humble and submissive. The Bible says that she obeyed her uncle when she was powerful and successful just as much as she did when she was a young girl growing up in his house. Esther's heart was tender and she was happy to be told what to do by her uncle, even when she was the queen of the country (Esther 2:20). God could trust this young woman. She was willing and obedient even when the stakes were high.

Stubborn symptoms!

Nehemiah 9:29 paints a picture of the symptoms of stubbornness. With an open mind and a humble heart, check yourself. It says, "They <u>acted proudly</u> and <u>did not heed</u> Your commandments, but <u>sinned against Your judgements</u>, which if a man does, he shall live by them. And they <u>shrugged their shoulders</u>, <u>stiffened their necks</u> and <u>would not hear.</u>"

You know best – You speak and behave as though you are very knowledgeable. You project an image of being right. You sometimes undermine the opinions of others and think very highly of your own abilities and opinions. The word 'proudly' here is best translated as presumptuously. You make assumptions and presume you are right. **"Yet they acted proudly"**

You won't rethink – There are times when you just don't want to listen to what people around you are saying. You are set on your course and you are determined not to be interrupted. **"They did not heed"**

You don't like taking orders – You are quick to turn down or reject the counsel of others when it directly contradicts your opinion or the decisions you have already made. You choose when to do what you're asked to do, even when those requests are made by people you respect. Left unchecked, stubbornness will develop into rebellion. Stubbornness says, "I want my way." So I resist obeying my God, leader, husband or boss. **"They sinned against Your judgments"**

You make excuses – You quickly dismiss a challenge to your character. You shrug your shoulders, telling yourself, "They don't know me as well as I know myself. They might mean well, but they're wrong." Perhaps even in a relaxed way, you make excuses to yourself. **"They shrugged their shoulders"**

You argue your point and dig your heels in – You are very quick to defend your point of view and to challenge those who challenge you. The more they present a different perspective, the stronger your position becomes - even when biblical counsel says you're off course. **"They stiffened their necks"**

You won't hear – It doesn't really matter what anyone else says. You will not listen to the views of others once your mind is made up. You probably think this is a great attribute, but it's a symptom of stubbornness. Great people need to be able to have their minds changed and their perspectives altered. **"They would not hear"**

What's the answer?

Be real - We should accept that we could be wrong. We have to acknowledge that we need to be told and then we need to become willing to be told. I don't know best, I do get it wrong and I don't always hear God as clearly as I think I do!

Bend - Let's expect to have our minds changed. We need to go into meetings with friends or leaders ready to be put right. We must be determined, but bendable. We need to submit to pivotal people because God works through lines of authority.

Confess - We need to acknowledge that we're stubborn, even if only occasionally. "Rebellion is as sinful as witchcraft and stubbornness as bad as worshipping idols." (1 Samuel 15:23b New Living Translation). We need to drive every trace of it out of our lives. The truth is that when we are stubborn, we are rebelling. We are lifting our opinions above those of others and idolising our own views. "I acknowledge my transgressions." (Psalm 51:3)

Listen - Now it's time to make a conscious effort to listen to the Holy Spirit through other people. We need to be humble enough to hear wisdom, irrespective of who it comes through.

"Because your heart was tender, and you humbled yourself before the Lord when you heard what I spoke..."
2 Kings 22:19

People with the propensity to be stubborn have the potential to become powerhouses in the hands of God. If you can stand fast in your determination yet become quick to listen, and if you remain tenacious but stop arguing, God can take that strong will and use it for His glory.

Prayer

Father God,

I realise that I have often been stubborn. When I make up my mind, I refuse to budge. I often want my own way. I am sorry. I want to be like putty in Your hands, not like stone that is difficult to shape.

I choose today to yield to You. I will submit to the people around me and in authority over me. I would rather risk making some wrong decisions with a right heart than risk falling because of a stubborn, hard heart.

Help me to be tender-hearted. Please change me and have Your way in my life.

In Jesus's name, I pray,

Amen.

Daily confessions to help you yield

You might find it useful to confess these Bible verses over your life. Personalise them so that instead of saying, "Your heart was tender and you humbled yourself before the Lord," you confess in prayer, "My heart is tender and I humble myself before the Lord…"

"Your heart was tender and you humbled yourself before the Lord…" 2 Kings 22:19

"Today if you will hear His voice, do not harden your hearts." Psalm 95:8

"Purify me from my sin for I recognize my rebellion." Psalm 51:2-3 (New Living Translation)

"The sacrifice You desire is a broken spirit. You will not reject a broken and contrite heart, O God." Psalm 51:17 (New Living Translation)

Chapter 7

It's just not fair

There are no two people in the world who are identical. Of the billions of men and women who have lived and died over countless generations, no individual has had the same fingerprints as another. Although so-called identical twins are born across the globe, no two people are in fact identical. Their smiles, walk, humour and expressions are different. There are no duplicates and there never will be. You are unique.

So why do we spend our lives measuring ourselves against people who are different? When I compare my job, my children, my ministry, my position, my life or my gifts, I may just be straying outside my business. God made me unique so how can I determine my success or failure by comparing myself with others?

Of course some comparison is perfectly healthy. We rummage through clothes in our favourite shop to find the garment we like the most. We compare prices to find the best deal. But comparison is a problem when it's combined with insecurity or selfishness. Then it can create a breeding ground for jealousy, rivalry and even covetousness. Because we make comparisons for much of the time, we all too easily develop bad habits that have the power to derail our destiny without us even realising.

Pushed out

Sophie was five when her sister, Rachel, was born. Until that time, she had been her mother's only child and the centre of her universe. The arrival of Rachel turned her world upside down and created a sense of rejection. It's not that her mother had actually pushed her away, but the shock of a newcomer in the house made Sophie feel unwanted. She compared the attention she and Rachel were receiving and felt less loved. It was not long before jealousy entered her heart. These things creep up very subtly so Sophie had no real idea what she was feeling in those early years. By the time her sister joined her at secondary school, the relationship was fraught with problems. Sophie always felt that Rachel was that little bit cleverer, prettier and generally more popular than her. She constantly compared herself with her little sister and competed with her for the spotlight. She even tried to be like her in some ways. But the envy didn't stop there. She would put Rachel down in front of her school friends, she would report her mistakes to her parents and she took every opportunity to embarrass or undermine her sister.

The jealousy that entered Sophie's heart hurt her more than anyone else. She ruined a relationship that she wanted to enjoy and feelings of resentment dominated much of her youth. As an adult, Sophie regretted that she had a sister she didn't really know.

Thank God that He is the Master Restorer. When Sophie faced the truth and asked God to heal the rejection she felt since Rachel's birth, she started on the road to recovery. She acknowledged the root and then dealt with the fruit of jealousy. Her relationship with Rachel began to improve.

It started at the very beginning

At the start of time, Satan tempted Eve to compare herself with God. The devil told her that if she ate fruit from the tree of the knowledge of good and evil she would become like God. She took the bait and allowed the thought to take root. Soon enough, she wanted something that belonged to someone else. That's the first example of covetousness in Scripture. Of course, God had already made her in His image. She was already like God. Nevertheless, she coveted God's gifting and ate the forbidden fruit.

Sibling rivalry

If God blesses my brother that doesn't mean He likes me any less. God's promotion of your sister doesn't mean He won't shower you with His goodness. So why do we see the blessing or success of others as a threat? Sadly, that's exactly what Adam and Eve's first child did.

Cain and his younger brother Abel both had a heart to serve the Lord. In fact, Cain was the first to bring an offering to God. He gave some of his crops and fruit and Abel brought God his first-born lambs. I believe the Lord had taught the sons of Adam about His heart and His ways. Perhaps God had explained the importance of giving your best. I'm sure He was about to teach them more. However, when Cain saw that his brother's offering was better, he was very upset.

God realised that Cain was angry so He explained to the young man that if he made the right choices, he would do well. I believe that God had great plans for Cain and wanted to test his heart. We always have a choice. When jealousy knocks at the door, we *can* drive it away:

> *"You will be accepted if you do what is right. But if you refuse to do what is right, then watch out! Sin is crouching at the door, eager to control you. But you must subdue it and be its master." Genesis 4:7 (New Living Translation)*

Cain gave in to jealousy's cravings and murdered his own flesh and blood. He couldn't handle the favour of God towards his brother and became history's first murderer.

Jealousy will always seek to hurt other people. It's not passive. It's compulsive and it craves retaliation. It might be an unkind comment, a whisper behind the back or a withdrawal of love. We can't accommodate envy without it infecting our attitudes and behaviour. I think the image of jealousy crouching at the door is a good one. If we let it in, we will pay the price.

Favouritism

It can be extremely painful if your father or mother prefers your brother or sister. Unfair treatment at home can take its toll and wound your heart. We see several examples of God's people being affected by favouritism. Jacob grew up knowing his dad adored his twin brother

Esau. Consequently, Jacob spent much of his early life trying to prove his self-worth. He probably envied Esau's relationship with their dad and felt inadequate at times.

Similarly, Jacob's sons were hurt by his own preferential love for Joseph. They were treated differently to the 'golden boy' and jealousy took root in their hearts. They probably felt that they were not good enough. Like Cain, they sought to destroy the one who was favoured.

An insecure heart can all too easily become a breeding ground for jealousy. When you are insecure, you are more likely to feel threatened when the spotlight is on someone else. You are more likely to compare yourself with other people.

When a leader or a boss prefers someone else, it can hurt us or make us feel rejected. If we give in to jealousy, it can eat us up inside and spoil everything. It's always best to resist the temptation to compare ourselves with someone else. We should remind ourselves that we are unique and special to God whilst rejoicing with others in their season of favour. It's an approach that will keep jealousy away.

Jealousy in leadership

King Saul was chosen by God. He was a handsome, gifted man. However, as we saw in previous chapters, he never dealt with insecurity. As a result, when people started to celebrate David's success, jealousy bit hard.

"So the women sang as they danced and said: 'Saul has slain his thousands and David his ten thousands.' Then

Saul was very angry and the saying displeased him and he said, 'They have ascribed to David ten thousands and to me they have ascribed only thousands. What more can he have but the kingdom?' So Saul eyed David from that day forward." 1 Samuel 18:7-9

Satan hounded Saul, determined to destroy his destiny. Jealousy was the weapon that finally worked. Verse nine in this passage actually means "Saul viewed David with suspicion from that day forward". Often when we are suspicious of the motives of others, we are actually assuming that they are thinking what we are thinking! Because we are jealous, we assume others are jealous. Because we feel threatened, we assume others feel threatened. David was not jealous of Saul's crown. It was Saul who envied David. Saul was suspicious, yet he was the only one who was guilty of suspect behaviour. It wasn't long before Saul became obsessed with killing David. Although Saul's jealousy hurt David, the real victim was Saul.

It was jealousy that drove the Pharisees to have Jesus put to death. They couldn't handle someone else being loved and respected by the masses. They were determined to remove the competition. His popularity incensed them to such an extent that they ordered His crucifixion. God is a God of knowledge and by Him our actions are weighed. When we harbour jealousy, it torments us and leaves us with feelings of injustice and judgment. It's horrible.

Because of insecurities, I used to compete for attention and recognition. Wherever I was and whatever I was doing, I would compete with the people around me.

I wanted to be more spiritual, more knowledgeable and more successful. If somebody I thought was on a level with me threatened my self-image, I would fight back with arguments and anecdotes that asserted my value. I wanted people to know that I was important. If I thought others were more important than me, it made me feel small.

As God was establishing me in ministry, I used to feel threatened by a particular friend and brother. As I sought to find my own place, I felt intimidated by his position. It was only as I became secure in God and aware of these issues that I was able to stop competing with my companion.

The Jewish worship leader Asaph shared a personal testimony about how he dealt with jealousy in one of the Psalms he wrote. Clearly, the devil was trying to use this to remove him from ministry and cut short his destiny:

> *"Truly God is good... to such as are pure in heart. But as for me, <u>my feet had almost stumbled; my steps had nearly slipped. For I was envious</u>..." Psalm 73:1-2*

In Hebrew, the word jealous means filled with emotion and passion. Jealousy has the potential to fill us with zeal. But it can propel our thoughts, words and actions towards our downfall. In fact, it is a test most of us will have to pass to reach the next level. You need to learn to see your friend or co-worker promoted to the position you were hoping for and rejoice with them. You need to learn to watch people around you achieve the status and success you dearly desire, and be glad for them. We have to capture jealous thoughts and put them to death.

The minute jealousy is given free reign, we need to repent. Until we can rejoice in someone else's season, we are not ready for our own season.

It feels horrible

The Psalmist Asaph described his feelings and thoughts as jealousy tried to dominate...

> *"Surely I have cleansed my heart in vain and washed my hands in innocence for all day long I have been plagued."*
> *Psalm 73:13-14*

What's the point of serving if I never get promoted? What's wrong with me? Why do others get opportunities? Why has he got his breakthrough when he hardly ever comes to church? Why has she got her miracle when she barely knows the Word? What's the point of praying and fasting?

These are the sorts of resentments we feel and painful questions we ask when we compare ourselves with others. The Psalmist went on to say:

> *"When I tried to understand this it was too painful for me until I went into the sanctuary of God." Psalm 73: 16-17*

The sad irony is that while we compare our walk with someone else's and wish for what they've got, our breakthrough is delayed.

So how should we handle the blessing that God pours out on those around us? Rejoice with those who do better than you and determine that you will be joyful and faithful. Pray that those you compete with will be raised to greater heights and glory. That will soon knock jealousy on the head! Be generous with your prayers and desires. Put the goals and aspirations of others above your own destiny. It will help you enormously. When the Psalmist put his focus back on the things of God, he was set free from envy's grip.

The spiritual root

The tenth commandment warns us not to look over our shoulder at what God has done for others. We need to be content with and grateful for what He has done for us.

> *"You shall not covet your neighbour's house, you shall not covet your neighbour's wife, nor his male servant, nor his female servant, nor his ox, nor his donkey, nor anything that is your neighbour's." Exodus 20:17*

If we look at something that belongs to someone else and want it for ourselves, that is covetousness. If we want their position, their promotion, their blessing, their job, their success or their house, we are directly opposing the tenth commandment.

You might say, "I'm just believing God to give me what they've got!" But the Bible says that the law of love fulfils all the old covenant commandments. If you love your neighbour as much as you love yourself, then you will be as happy when they do well as when you succeed. The opposite of covetousness is generosity. The opposite of jealousy is loving-kindness. When you really love your neighbour as yourself, there will be no room for jealousy or covetousness.

I remember travelling through London with a prophet. I saw some beautiful houses and commented that I'd like one. He replied that he wouldn't even believe God for a house that was currently occupied. He refused to seek to own something that belonged to someone else. Instead, he would describe his heart's desire to the Lord.

The problem with jealousy...

Jealousy feels awful and makes us behave badly. Ultimately, it will rob us of our destiny. These are some of its effects in our lives:

It makes us oppose the people we envy. When we see God blessing or promoting someone else, Satan tries to stir up envy. The devil will use us to oppose the very people God is honouring. We might argue, become awkward, be slow to support them or raise concerns. In Acts, when the leaders saw the multitudes gathering to hear Paul, they were filled with envy (Acts 13:45) so they argued against his message and contradicted him. Questioning or debating with the person we envy is a common consequence of jealousy.

It disqualifies people from ministry. When Satan tries to exclude us from positions of responsibility and leadership, one of the weapons he will use is jealousy. If it's the desire of your heart to serve God and to lead His people in one way or another, I encourage you to watch your heart. When Moses's father-in-law advised the man of God to raise up a team of leaders, he warned him not to put jealous people in authority:

"Select from all the people able men, such as fear God, men of truth, <u>hating covetousness,</u> and place such over them to be rulers of thousands, rulers of hundreds, rulers of fifties and rulers of tens." Exodus 18:21

It's destructive. We saw with Cain, Joseph's brothers and Saul that jealousy seeks to destroy. The spirit of jealousy tries to sabotage both its object as well as the person who lets it into their heart. Cain's destiny was ruined, Joseph's brothers suffered guilt and fear for years and Saul lost his life and his legacy. Jealousy is a killer: "Surely resentment destroys the fool, and jealousy kills the simple." Job 5:2 (New Living Translation)

It opens the door to sickness. All too easily, jealousy hardens our hearts. We start to resent those we have envied. This is a problem because envy can ultimately cause physical as well as spiritual problems. "Envy is rottenness to the bones" Proverbs 14:30

It produces hate. If we allow jealousy to grow in our hearts then it will spread and can produce hate. We end up detesting the person that makes us feel jealous. They make us feel badly treated. They have what we want and we can't stand it. Joseph's brothers were so jealous of the love their father showed to the golden boy that it soon became hate: "But when his brothers saw that their father loved him more than all his brothers, they hated him and could not speak a kind word to him." Genesis 37:4

It can make us behave cruelly. Jealousy can make us do unkind things. Without realising it, you put a friend down who has just been promoted. You refuse to support someone who is getting married because you have been waiting for a partner for years. Jealousy can make good people do awful things. Joseph's brothers felt justified in treating their brother abominably. They threw him into a ditch, ignored his cries for mercy, then sat beside the pit and feasted! "We saw the anguish of his soul when he pleaded with us and we would not hear." (Genesis 42:21). The coldness of heart of these soon-to-be leaders is hard to imagine. You may be more self-controlled than Joseph's brothers, but while jealousy dominates, you will feel the urge to be harsh or unkind also: "Jealousy is cruel as the grave: the coals are coals of fire, which have a most vehement flame." Song of Songs 8:6.

We can see jealousy's harmful effects in our lives and in the lives of the people around us. It's time to deal with this problem at its root and evict it from our thoughts, hearts and lives.

A new outlook

I encourage you to renew your mind and change the way you think. If you constantly compare yourself with other people, it's time to stop. It is an exhausting and self-destructive trait. The Bible tells us to take captive every thought. Each time you find yourself making an unhelpful comparison, reject that thought and instead start to pray for the blessing of that brother or sister. In so doing, you are punishing comparison and practising generosity. You are arresting selfishness and releasing loving-kindness. Make a habit of speaking words of blessing over their lives.

> *"For <u>we dare not class ourselves or compare ourselves</u> with those who commend themselves. But they, measuring themselves by themselves and comparing themselves among themselves, are not wise"* 2 Corinthians 10:12

The Bible always says it like it is. Although making a comparison is a common thing to do, it is not wise! Don't measure your success against the achievements of others. Seek to be your own best, not your brother's best.

God spoke to Abraham in Genesis twelve and promised to make his name great. I remember asking the Lord about this. Why would our wonderful Saviour want to instil ambition in the hearts of His people? What God showed me was very helpful. He never promised to make Abraham the *greatest*. He promised to make Abraham *great*. Abraham's success was not dependent on his rising higher than others. Abraham's success was dependent on him becoming *his* best. The Lord's plan is that every one of us will be great. Only One is the greatest - that's God's job!

So how do we deal with jealousy?

We need to hate jealousy and refuse it in our lives. The more we bless people who have what we want, the more we will remove jealousy from our soul. Let's look at how to evict it from our everyday lives.

Recognise it's a problem. Some 'sins' are harder to own up to than others. There's something about jealousy that doesn't sound good. Remember that it's a very basic human issue that most of us will have to deal with at some time or another. Truth and then confession is always the starting point. Tell the Lord that you have been jealous and ask Him to help you become free. If you believe it is rooted in rejection or insecurity, tell Him and ask Him to heal you.

Make a decision and then be accountable. If there are certain people who you often find yourself competing with or comparing yourself to, it's time to stop. It's only harming you and damaging your relationship with that brother or sister. There are certain sins that try to become part of our identity. I call them 'personality sins'. This is when certain attitudes or behaviours become engrained in our lives. To break those patterns requires much more effort than dealing with a problem at the periphery. I always find someone to confess my 'personality sins' to. If jealousy has been a big problem for you, ask God to show you why and tell a close, trusted friend.

Don't do it anymore. God's word says: "Do not let your heart envy" (Proverbs 23:17). This verse reassures me that you and I can stop jealousy in its tracks. If a jealous thought comes as a seed, don't allow it to take root in your heart. Kick the thought out and replace it with a generous, loving prayer. If you feel a pang of envy, don't act on it. Instead, say or do something to celebrate the person of whom you're jealous. "Make no provision for the flesh, to fulfill its lusts." Romans 13:14

Be content and grateful. There was a season when I knew I was poised for something new. I had received prophecies and assurances that God was about to launch me into the next phase of my life and ministry. The desire to move on started to affect my attitude. I began to feel irritated and bored. I spoke to my husband about my frustration. He smiled and said, "You need more contentment in your life." Within a couple of days, my heart was right again and I was thanking God for His faithfulness. I believe I passed a test that opened the door to the next season. Paul the apostle said that he had learned to be content in every situation, whether in lack or in plenty, whether he was up or down. Contentment is a sign of gratitude to God for what He has ALREADY done. Work at contentment in your life and make thanksgiving a daily exercise. "Let your conduct be without covetousness; be content with such things as you have." (Hebrews 13:5)

Be secure. Remember that you don't need to be like anyone else. You don't need a position, a job title, a husband or a wife, a child or a talent to feel good about yourself. You are unique and God loves the way He made you. Join Paul in confessing: "I am what I am by the favour of God." 1 Corinthians 15:10

Prayer

Father God,

Thank You for everything You have done for me. Thank You for the plans You have for me. Thank You that I am unique and that You love me. I don't need to compare myself with others anymore. Instead, I seek to be my own personal best.

Where I have been jealous and grasping, please forgive me, Lord. When I have wanted someone else's position, success or blessing, please forgive me, Lord. When I have been argumentative, unkind or abrupt towards those I have envied, please forgive me, Lord. I am sorry for every occasion I have envied or coveted and I ask You to change my heart.

I am grateful for all You have done in my life. Thank You for every blessing You have given me. Thank You for loving me and saving me.

I rejoice with those who are succeeding (*be specific and name people*) and I pray that You will promote and prosper my friends and companions more and more.

I choose to be content. I am grateful for my life and I give You all the glory.

In Jesus's name,

Amen.

Daily confessions to help you become content

You might find it useful to confess these Bible verses over your life. Personalise them so that instead of saying,

"Be content with such things as you have," you confess in prayer, "I am content with what I have."

"Let your conduct be without covetousness; be content with such things as you have." Hebrews 13:5

"Godliness accompanied with contentment (that contentment which is a sense of inward sufficiency) is great and abundant gain." 1 Timothy 6:6 (Amplified)

"I am what I am by the favour of God..." 1 Corinthians 15:10

Chapter 8

Lengthening your fuse

People express anger in different ways, but it's the same emotion. Some internalise rage and retreat. You shut the door and allow your thoughts to fester. You don't let anyone in. Others become impatient, agitated and snappy. You bark at people around you and make sure everyone knows you are cross. Some are huffy or moody. Another group of people explodes. Perhaps it doesn't happen when your anger is just simmering away. But when it reaches a crescendo, you blow up and everybody around you knows it. Voices are raised, strong words are spoken, doors slam, and all the rest of it.

Then there's the kind of anger that is directed towards one particular person. You might be happy and enjoying life until their name is mentioned or their number flashes up on your phone. Perhaps they have done something that really wound you up. They think they have the right to treat people without due consideration. Maybe they are self-centred or immature. Perhaps they are downright rude. All you know is that at the mention of their name, you react or recoil. You rehearse their wrongs and lose your peace. You may hardly utter a word about them or you might regularly express your indignation. Either way, anger towards that brother or sister bubbles within.

The dictionary definition of anger is an intense feeling of displeasure. It's when we react to the attitudes, words or actions of others or to our circumstances. We feel agitated, incredulous, incensed or annoyed.

It doesn't necessarily matter how we 'do' anger. We just need to know that it always affects our hearts and lives. It can wound our relationships and the people around us. It can harm us as well.

> *"Be <u>angry</u> and do not sin. Do not let the sun go down on your <u>wrath</u> nor give place to the devil." Ephesians 4:26-27*

There are two different words used here for anger. The first word means provocation. In other words, the Bible is telling us that we will all be provoked to anger. Situations will arise that aggravate us. However, with the help of the Holy Spirit, we can learn not to respond in a carnal way.

The second word for anger means exasperation, indignation or fury. This is when we have taken the bait, we have been provoked and anger has taken hold in our hearts. We meditate on our complaint, revisit the injustice and indignation builds.

It's the second kind of anger that is dangerous. The same verse in the New Living Translation helps us to understand why:

> *"Don't sin by letting anger <u>control</u> you. Don't let the sun go down while you are still angry, for <u>anger gives a foothold to the devil.</u>" Ephesians 4:26-27 (New Living Translation)*

Anger wants to take control of our feelings and thoughts so we must fight against it. We must prevent it from dominating our attitudes and behaviour. Love always finds a way to be patient and kind.

The Bible tells us that Satan can get a foothold in our lives if we allow that kind of anger to remain, even for a few hours. When we harbour anger, we can accidentally invite the devil to come and make himself at home in one of the rooms of our hearts. We literally give him a key to our life.

Sure, your son may have been rude yet again. Yes, your wife may have got yet another parking fine. Your girlfriend may have broken your MP3 player and your colleague may have taken the credit for your work. Someone may have overstepped the mark and been rude or selfish. But the Bible tells us that the devil sees anger as an opportunity. He loves to provoke us and surround us with injustice or unfair treatment so that he can find a way into our lives. It's therefore our job to practice love because love is not easily provoked (1 Corinthians 13:5).

But doesn't God get angry?

You may be saying, "When Jesus cleansed the temple, He became very angry." Yes, Jesus was angry. However, He did not sin. He was upset, yet He did not yield to provocation. When He was cleansing the temple (Matthew 21:13), He spoke to the people rather than shouting at them. One of the fruits of the Spirit is self-control and Jesus never lacked any fruit. He never 'lost it'.

It is interesting to note that Jesus shouted a few times, but not when he was angry. Two mentions of Jesus 'crying aloud' can be found in the gospel of John: when He preached about the coming baptism of the Holy Spirit (John 7:37) and when He commanded Lazarus to rise from the dead (John 11:43).

Even in the Old Testament, we see self-control and love at the heart of God's anger. As He pronounced His judgment and wrath against the people of Israel through the prophet Jeremiah, He also reassured them of the coming restoration (Jeremiah 29-33). God never has and never will 'lose' His temper. His anger only lasts for a moment and is designed to bring loving correction to His people. His favour lasts for a lifetime and His mercy endures forever. He can switch between talking about His anger and His compassion because anger never overtakes Him.

Disqualified by anger

Jacob prayed for each of his sons before he died, blessing them one by one. However, he refused to bless Simeon and Levi and instead pronounced a curse because they had allowed anger to provoke them to violence. For Jacob, this was enough for their destinies to be cut short:

> *"Let not my soul enter their council; Let not my honour be united to their assembly; For in their anger they slew a man and in their self-will they hamstrung an ox. <u>Cursed be their anger, for it is fierce; and their wrath, for it is cruel! I will divide them in Jacob and scatter them in Israel</u>." Genesis 49:6-7*

Moses had a temper. I believe that God wanted to deal with him about his anger. On one occasion, Moses returned from a glorious encounter with God to discover that the people of Israel had backslidden and were worshipping a golden calf. He was carrying the stone tablets that God had personally engraved with the ten commandments. Moses was so angry at the sin of the people that he threw the tablets on the ground and they broke.

"So Moses's anger became hot, and he cast the tablets out of his hands and broke them at the foot of the mountain." Exodus 32:19b

God showed Moses His love and patience by rewriting the commandments on new stones. Maybe the Lord was trying to show him how not to sin in the face of provocation. Perhaps He was trying to demonstrate the patience and endurance of love.

However, it was anger that eventually stopped Moses fulfilling his destiny. The people were complaining again and asking for water. When God told Moses to speak to the rock and provide the people with a drink, he called everyone together and gave them a piece of his mind:

"Listen, you rebels!" he shouted. "Must we bring you water from this rock?" Then Moses raised his hand and struck the rock…" Numbers 20:10-11 (New Living Translation)

Moses was provoked by the stubbornness of the people. But, rather than displaying self-control, he blew up:

"Because they defied God yet again, Moses exploded and lost his temper." Psalm 106:33 (Message Bible)

This outburst cost Moses the final chapter of God's plan for his life. Instead of leading God's people into the promised land, Moses died in the wilderness. God would not allow Moses to finish his mission because he lashed out in anger.

If we are going to fulfil our potential, we will have to learn to conquer anger. There are certain places God will not take us until we have dealt with moods and rage. The Lord needs to be able to trust us.

Anger's impact

Perhaps you were raised by people who turned at the flick of a switch. Maybe you have experienced the rage of family or friends. I used to freeze around people who had outbursts of rage. Something about another human being losing it used to render me powerless. I couldn't think about what they might be going through because their anger filled me with fear. I would tremble inside.

"Wrath is cruel and anger a torrent." Proverbs 27:4

When someone explodes at you or near you it can be a very frightening experience. The verse above compares anger with an overwhelming flood. I have been caught in the waves when the sea is rough. The ocean's power can knock you over. Before you're able to get up again, you are sucked back down by the next breaker. Like an outburst of rage, it is horrible.

When I was a child, I went to play at a friend's house. They had a huge dog. You could have mistaken it for a small horse! One day, my friend and I were playing in the lounge when her father marched in and yelled at the top of his voice, "Get out of this house!" I ran as fast as my little legs would carry me, shaking and trembling with fear. I then discovered that the reprimand was directed at the dog! I looked and felt really silly, but it illustrated an important point: it doesn't matter who an outburst is directed at - everyone nearby is affected.

Solomon's wife was wounded by the angry reactions of her siblings. She carried that hurt into adult life:

> *"My brothers were angry with me; they forced me to care for their vineyards, so I couldn't care for myself..." Song of Songs 1:6b*

If you have been hurt by the physical or verbal violence of another person, you will need to ask the Lord to heal you. He is the Master Restorer. Many people who were raised by parents or guardians who regularly exploded with rage go on to express anger in the same way. The very patterns that shocked and wounded us as we grew up can become second nature to us in adult life. To become free from our own anger we need to be healed from the effects of the anger of others.

If you experienced a harsh upbringing and reading this chapter is bringing it all flooding back, I encourage you to go to God in prayer. Tell Him about the experiences you suffered in detail. Explain how those events made you feel and ask Him to heal you of the pain you suffered. Ask

Him to restore what was damaged. Why not make time straight away to bring this to the Lord? Pain is always better outside rather than inside us and a key way of releasing it is by talking. The Bible says that on the cross, Jesus carried our sorrows. Give the bitter memories of the past to Him by telling the Lord out loud what you went through. Then ask Him to heal you in the depths of your heart.

Tell tale signs

The Hebrew for anger is interesting. It literally means face, nostril or nose. It is the expression used for strong breathing. In other words, it is when anger has stopped being just a feeling and when you and I have let it out. The word suggests it's when anger has become visible. I can tell when my nine year old daughter is angry as her nose starts to wrinkle. When I am getting cross, my face is more stern than usual and my eyes are fiery. When we have lost control of anger, it usually appears somewhere on our faces or in our gestures. Let's look at the different ways in which people express anger.

Temper, temper

If you know that you have the propensity to explode when rage builds within, I encourage you to seek God's help. As we saw from Proverbs 27:4, when anger breaks, it can be cruel and frightening for the people around us. You are never at your best when you are out of control. And while you have an unpredictable temper, God may need to delay the blessings He has for you. The Bible says that as a man thinks in his heart, so he is (Proverbs 23:7). The beginning of change will be a change of heart and mind. If you were raised by violent men or women, it will be really important to ask God to heal you. Ask Him to set you free from the pain of the past. Ask Him to restore your heart.

Now it's time to recognise that there is a problem and to acknowledge the impact that it has on other people. Ask God to change your view of yourself. Don't see yourself the way you were. Allow Him to paint a fresh picture of yourself with more love, greater patience and new self-control. It may take time, but keep your eyes on God's ability to heal and transform.

Not my problem

I hated rage and that probably hoodwinked me into thinking I was blameless in this area. I believed for a long time that I was a very gentle person. I remember one day having a frank conversation with an employee who was thanking me for being a good manager. I appreciated her gratitude and commented that I thought I was probably quite a gentle leader. "Gentle?" she asked quizzically. "Er, you're fair and supportive, but I wouldn't use the word gentle." I was surprised. I believed I was a calm person. I rarely shouted, hardly ever slammed doors and never punched walls. Nonetheless, my anger would rear its head in other ways.

Sharp and snappy

You might not yell, but perhaps you snap. Maybe you become irritable and make pointed comments designed to put down or hurt your 'opponent'.

"There is one who speaks like the piercings of a sword."
Proverbs 12:18

You might go about your business more loudly than before and shut the doors with an extra bang. You want to make sure that your anger is advertised and the people around you suffer. After all, you are suffering. That's still unrestrained anger.

"A soft answer turns away wrath but <u>a harsh word stirs up anger.</u>" Proverbs 15:1

When we're angry, we usually want to provoke those around us. Now that we have given in and become angry, we often taunt others so that they become angry too.

Silent treatment

You may be one of those who never shout and rarely snap, but who simply push away the people who anger you. You revisit your complaints. You brush off your opponent's requests for communication or pleas for mercy. You keep the world away and yourself to yourself. If it's your spouse who you're angry with, you go to bed thinking, "No sex for you tonight!"

"A man who isolates himself seeks his own desire, he rages against all wise judgement." Proverbs 18:1

I know from personal experience how painful it can be when someone shuts you out. You desperately want to connect with the one you love, but you are in the doghouse and you have to wait until they are ready. The rejection is like a punch in the guts.

It's fine until they show up!

Perhaps you recognise that your anger tends to be directed towards one or two people in particular. You can't stand the way they behave or treat those you love. You think someone needs to put them in their place. Just picturing their face makes your heart beat faster and your blood curdle. You would really love to remove them from your world, but that's not allowed, is it? You may even have imaginary conversations where you tell them what you really think. You feel a tightness just thinking about them.

Called to ministry?

God has high expectations of those He raises in pulpit ministries. If you know that God has called you to preach or teach the Word of God, there is a particular need to deal with anger:

> *"And the servant of the Lord must not be quarrelsome (fighting and contending). Instead, he must be kindly to everyone and mild-tempered [preserving the bond of peace]" 2 Timothy 2:24 (Amplified)*

God asks every minister or would-be preacher to work on his or her temper. I have to watch irritability in my life. All too easily, when things aren't going to plan, I get frustrated with the people around me. Recently, I arrived at our church premises to find a bottle of bleach and a vacuum cleaner left unattended near one of our children's classes. We pay a great deal of attention to health and safety. We don't want anyone to get hurt so we have strict policies. I felt annoyed and my flesh wanted to snap at the culprit. Instead, I reminded myself that she was a volunteer who was cleaning out of the kindness of her heart. I spoke clearly but gently about the situation. If I had snapped, I could have hurt her feelings. I am learning to hold back impatience and replace it with kindness. We need to remember that we are Christ's ambassadors and we represent Him.

> *"A bishop then must be blameless, the husband of one wife, temperate, sober-minded, of good behaviour..."* **1 Timothy 3:2**

Being temperate means curbing our desires and impulses. It is another word for self-control or moderation. God expects His servants to show great self-control, always considering the wellbeing and emotional state of the people around us.

Role models

Nehemiah learned how to master his emotions. There are several examples of him doing this. Here's one:

> *"I became very angry when I heard their outcry and these words. After serious thought, I rebuked the nobles and rulers, and said to them..." Nehemiah 5:6-7*

When the behaviour of God's people outraged Nehemiah, he used self-control and stopped to think about the situation. Before doing anything, he gave the matter serious contemplation. He did not shout or react. He paused for some time and then acted wisely. We can do what Nehemiah did. When we are provoked, we can take time out to think things through calmly. It's hard, but it's well worth it.

For James and John's destinies to be fulfilled, God had to change these young men. When they came to Jesus, He called them "Sons of thunder" (Mark 3:17). Thunder is loud, sudden and frightening to many. By the time Jesus had finished with them, John had a new reputation - no longer for outbursts - but for love. And James gladly gave his life for the gospel.

How do I get out of here?

Awareness is the first step to freedom. Become aware of your reactions and attitudes. Be honest with yourself about the way you behave and don't make excuses when you get it wrong.

Remember that anger starts with provocation. When we are provoked, the natural reaction is to jerk the knee. We need to learn to resist our pre-programmed responses. This verse provides some simple principles that can help us to overcome anger in our lives:

> *"Let every man be __quick to hear__ [a ready listener], __slow to speak, slow to take offence__ and __to get angry__. For man's anger does not promote the righteousness God [wishes and requires]." James 1:19-20 (Amplified)*

Listen

It's amazing how the flesh loves to be heard: "I want my way and I want it now! I don't like what you've done or how you've done it so I don't want to hear anything more from you!" In contrast, the Bible tells us to listen to other people. That means we do this as carefully when we don't want to hear what they have to say as when we do. Simply taking the time to listen and making a point of trying to understand what other people are saying will help a great deal. It will slow down your reactions and turn your attention from your own indignation to the viewpoint of another.

Don't speak

What we say is very powerful. The truth is that we probably believe what we say more than what others say. When we are angry, we are normally full of talk. Whether it actually comes out of your mouth as a rant or stays locked up within is not relevant. If you can learn to slow down the argument it will help. The Bible says that love believes the best. It doesn't jump to conclusions, but it is patient and kind. Try to intercept anger before it produces a torrent of indignation in your own mind.

> *"Be angry and do not sin, <u>meditate within your heart on your bed and be still</u>. Offer the sacrifices of righteousness and put your trust in the Lord." Psalm 4:4-5*

Verse four in the Amplified says: "Be angry and sin not; commune with your own heart upon your bed and be silent (sorry for the things you say in your heart). Selah [pause, and calmly think of that]."

We need to refuse the rant that is trying to break forth and allow our hearts the chance to choose love. The Bible encourages us to 'put on' love and to walk in it. See that brother or sister as a child of God who therefore deserves your kindness. Overlook their sin. That's what love does. Draw upon the limitless, gracious and merciful love of the Father. Love with His love.

Take time

When we are angry, we need time out. For some, that means counting to ten or quietly leaving the room. We need to take control so that anger doesn't take control of us. We need to calm down. The New Living Translation puts Psalm 4:4 like this: "Don't sin by letting anger control you. Think about it overnight and remain silent." That's not the silent treatment - it's quietness!

The 'sacrifice' mentioned in verse five is choosing to be loving and righteous when you feel like reacting. It's deciding to be patient and kind when you feel like demanding justice, shouting or shutting down. When we resist the provocation of anger, we are bringing a sacrifice to the Lord. He will receive our offering of loving- kindness with gladness. He will be proud of us.

Don't take offence

The verse in James says, "Be slow to take offence." You might say that you don't get offended, you just get cross. Offence is simply when we hold anger in our hearts. You may say, "I'm just upset with my wife for making me late." In reality, you might be storing anger on the inside. We like to use all sorts of words to disguise offence: "I'm not offended, I'm just disappointed...I'm not holding a grudge, I'm just cross...I'm not angry, I'm just really upset...I'm not resentful, I'm annoyed!" These are just different words for the same heart issue. If we hold onto any one of these negative attitudes for any length of time, offence will take root in our hearts.

"A brother offended is harder to win than a strong city and contentions are like the bars of a castle." Proverbs 18:19

Once offence finds a home in our hearts, it clouds our judgement, poisons our hearts and robs our joy. We become convinced we are right and close our ears to other people's perspectives. Offence makes us stumble and fall in our relationship with God (Mark 4:17).

Slow down

We need to learn to lengthen our fuses! We need slower reaction times and to stop jumping to judgments or conclusions.

"People with understanding control their anger; a hot temper shows great foolishness." Proverbs 14:29 (New Living Translation)

Scripture tells us we are acting foolishly when we snap and react. The Amplified Bible talks about a 'short spirit'. Today we would say a short fuse. Having a short fuse is not the sign of a smart person, as the world might have you think. It's an indication of someone who has not yet won the battle of self-control.

"Stop being angry. Turn from your rage. Do not lose your temper – it only leads to harm." Psalm 37:8 (New Living Translation)

Rage and anger will always harm someone. It will usually injure the person who is annoyed and very often their 'opponent' too. It's time to deal with anger.

The truth

God has great plans for your life and it's time to take hold of every bit of potential you possess. Moses's destiny was cut short as a result of anger and Simeon and Levi were denied their rightful blessings because they lashed out. For you and I to accomplish our best, we need to learn to control our emotions.

"Whoever has no rule over his own spirit is like a city broken down without walls." Proverbs 25:28

If I have no control over my temper or my moods, I'm like a broken city with no defence against enemy attack. You and I need to be in control of our own spirits if we are going to be all that God intended us to be.

"A fool vents his feelings but a wise man holds them back." Proverbs 29:11

If you have little or no control over your emotions or your moods, it's time to be honest and seek God's help. The verse in Proverbs twenty five says you're broken, which means you need fixing. If you know that your emotions are all over the place, ask God to forgive you for where you have gone wrong. Ask Him to start a new work in you. One of the fruits of the Spirit is self-control. If you are God's child then you have His Spirit. Draw on His Spirit and ask for more self-control in your life. The more you work at self-control, the better at it you will become.

"He who is slow to anger is better than the mighty and he who rules his spirit than he who takes a city." Proverbs 16:32

When you feel anger stirring, make a decision not to give in. Your spirit belongs to you and your emotions are your responsibility. It's time to take charge! My emotions used to be all over the place. I was like a yo-yo and it was an awful way to live. I can tell you from personal experience that starting to apply self-control is hard, but it feels great when you begin to make progress. You can change with God's power.

Let it go

I have learned a great deal from being a parent. One such lesson is about choosing my battles. Does it really matter if my daughter goes out of the house dressed in clashing colours? It's far more important that she doesn't lie than she finishes her last few potatoes. This principle helps in other areas of life. Sometimes, I have to learn to let things go, even if a person is in the wrong. My reaction might be more of an issue than someone else's transgression. Learn to release issues in other people's lives that are bothering you. Learn to overlook wrongdoing. It will take a lot of stress out of your life.

"The discretion of a man makes him slow to anger and his glory is to overlook a transgression." Proverbs 19:11

I want to keep Satan out of my life and I'm sure you do too. Allow God to do a wonderful work of love and patience and to make your life more peaceful as a result.

"Let all bitterness and indignation and wrath (passion, rage, bad temper) and resentment (anger, animosity) and quarrelling (brawling, clamour, contention) and slander (evil-speaking, abusive or blasphemous language) be banished from you, with all malice (spite, ill will, or baseness of any kind). And become useful and helpful and kind to one another, tenderhearted (compassionate, understanding, loving-hearted), forgiving one another [readily and freely], as God in Christ forgave you."
Ephesians 4:31-32 (Amplified)

Let's allow the tenderness of God to work in us. Let's allow the love of Christ to constrain us from harsh or hard-hearted behaviour. Just as Christ transformed John from a son of thunder to a disciple of love, God can change you and me.

Prayer

Father God,

Thank You for showing me how anger has affected my life. I recognise that I have allowed it to take root in different ways. *(Now tell the Lord how anger has had its way in your heart and where it took root, if you know.)*

I ask You to forgive me for holding anger in my heart. I choose today to let it go. I choose today to overlook the wrongs of others. We are all human and we are all allowed to make mistakes. Instead of dwelling on the sins of my brother/sister/mother, etc, I now look at the condition of my own heart and life.

I want to be free from all anger and I desire to become like You - full of love, patience and self-control.

Fill me afresh with Your Spirit, Oh Lord, I pray.

In Jesus's name,

Amen.

Daily confessions to help you conquer anger

You might find it useful to confess these Bible verses over your life. Personalise them so that instead of saying, "You must all be quick to listen, slow to speak, and slow to get angry. Human anger does not produce the righteousness God desires," you confess in prayer, "I am quick to listen, slow to speak and slow to get angry. My anger does not produce the righteousness God desires."

"You must all be quick to listen, slow to speak and slow to get angry. Human anger does not produce the righteousness God desires." James 1:19-20 (New Living Translation)

"He who is slow to anger is better than the mighty and he who rules his spirit than he who takes a city." Proverbs 16:32

"Love is patient and kind. Love is not jealous or boastful or proud or rude. It does not demand its own way. It is not irritable, and it keeps no record of being wronged." 1 Corinthians 13:4-5

In Closing

By God's grace, you will be experiencing greater freedom, peace and purity than when you started to read this book. I encourage you to stay in this attitude of humility and self-awareness so that the Lord can change you to be more like Him, day by day. The Bible says that we are changed from one degree of glory to the next. We're on a journey. Don't worry at all if you're not there yet. None of us is.

Just remember that your heart is your greatest asset. Take time to look after it and to protect it. Keeping your heart pure is your responsibility. Forging your future is God's.

Would you like to
invite Jesus into your heart?

If you would like to ask Jesus to become the Lord of your life, I would be honoured to lead you in a simple prayer. The Bible says that God loves you and that Jesus wants to draw close:

> *"Behold I stand at the door and knock. If anyone hears My voice and opens the door, I will come in." Revelation 3:20*

If you would like to know Jesus as your friend, Lord and Saviour, the first step is asking. Pray this prayer:

Dear Lord,

I know that You love me and have a good plan for my life. I ask You to come into my heart today and be my Lord. I give my life to You and ask You to lead me in Your ways from now on.

In Jesus's name,

Amen.

If you have prayed this prayer for the first time, it will be important to tell a Christian friend and find a good church. Just as a newborn baby needs nourishment and care, so you and I need the support of other believers as we start our new life as a follower of Jesus Christ.

You can listen free to Bible messages that will help build your faith at www.harvestchurch.org.uk. You can also follow us on twitter @londonharvest and you can become a friend of Harvest Church London or Jo Naughton on Facebook.

About the author

Together with her husband Paul, Jo Naughton pastors Harvest Church in London, England. Jo is used by God nationally and internationally to minister healing and restoration and to bring truth and clarity to men and women about everyday issues. Paul and Jo have two children, Benjamin and Abigail.

For more information about Harvest Church London or Jo Naughton, visit: www.harvestchurch.org.uk or jonaughton.com.

Also by this author

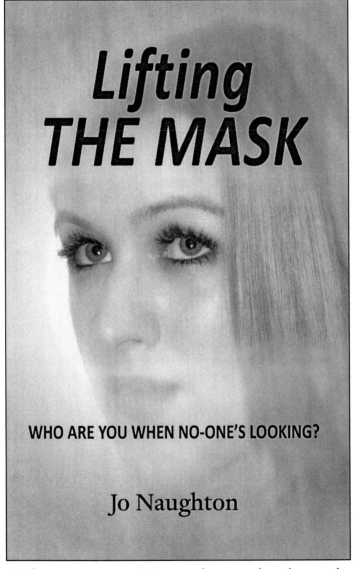

Lifting THE MASK

WHO ARE YOU WHEN NO-ONE'S LOOKING?

Jo Naughton

To buy your copy, visit www.harvestchurch.org.uk.

Lightning Source UK Ltd.
Milton Keynes UK
UKOW05f0738281114

242283UK00001B/27/P